How to Write

a

Bitboard

Chess Engine

FM Bill Jordan

HOW TO WRITE A BITBOARD CHESS ENGINE
First edition. Jan, 2020.
Updated November 2025
Copyright © 2020 FM Bill Jordan.
Written by FM Bill Jordan.

Table of Contents

Introduction

Who is this book for?

Anyone who is curious to learn about how a chess program works.

Programming students who wish to broaden their programming experience.

Chess players who would like to learn new things about chess.

Anyone who may be interested in developing a chess engine for fun.

My other programming books include:

- *The Joy of Chess Programming*
- *How to Write a Chess Program*
- *How to write a JavaScript Chess Engine*
- *Advanced Chess Programming*

If you have any suggestions or anything that needs correcting, please contact me at **swneerava@gmail.com**.

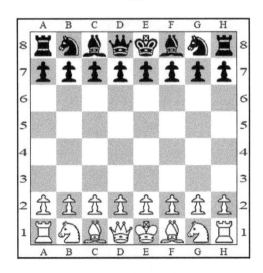

What is this book?

This book includes the source code for a bitboard chess engine. It's designed to be easy to understand while playing a reasonable game. You have the possibility of downloading the source code and creating an executable program. You can also download the **.exe** file and run the program. Alternatively you may just want to enjoy the book.

The engine can play a human, against itself or it can play other engines using a program such as *Arena* or the older *Winboard* program. Arena and Winboard are programs that allow different engines to play each other. They can be downloaded for free.

Program features

Don't panic if you are not familiar with some of the following terms.

The engine can generate all legal moves, including the *en passant* capture, castling and pawn promotion.

It can recognise the end of a game by:

- Checkmate.
- Stalemate.
- Triple repetition.
- The fifty move rule.
- Insufficient material.

The engine has a *hash table*.

It evaluates positions in terms of:

- Material.
- Piece position.
- Weak pawns.
- Passed pawns.
- King safety.

It searches the game tree with a classic Alpha-Beta search. It has features and concepts you will learn about including the following:

- Deepening iteration.
- Beta cutoffs.
- Extensions.
- Reductions.
- Quiescence search.

Moves are ordered as well as possible to reduce the amount of searching that needs to be done. Methods include:

- Hash table lookup.
- MV-LA
- History moves.

Other features include:

- Display of the principal variation.
- Display of number of positions which are searched each second.
- Ability to load positions to see what the engine would play.

How Are Chess Programs Written?

Most computer chess engines are written in the C or C++ computer programming languages. The older C language is a subset of the C++ language. It ultimately makes little difference whether C or C++ is used.

C++ features such as classes etc. can be used, though they are not necessary.

My bitboard engine is written in C++. It is written in the style of a C program. Chess engines do not need C++ classes. Chess engines can be written in other languages. C++ is popular because it is very fast. Speed is important for a chess engine. Many languages such as Java, Python, JavaScript, ActionScript etc. look similar to C/C++ so if you familiar with any of these you are well placed to understand the code.

Strong playing programs are difficult to write from scratch. Current engine strength is the result of many decades of an enormous amount of development time.

Program Chess Code

Even if do not know anything about programming at all, it still be be of interest to look at the source code. Source code consists of plain text files that can be edited or read with a program such as Windows Notepad.

Even if you know very little about programming, if you have a compiler and can learn how to compile a program and use it with Winboard, you may still be able to tinker with the code. For example, you may tinker with the evaluation. If you can find where the evaluation function is in the source code, you can tinker with the scores and test the effect on its playing strength and style.

How does an engine work?

The engine generates all possible moves from a given position. It calculates a score for each position. Everything is *quantified* (reduced to numbers). Material, king safety, pawn structure, piece mobility etc. can all be reduced to numbers. If it was only searching one move ahead, it would select the move with the highest score.

It then searches the new positions arising from each each of these moves, starting with the most promising. It selects the best line of play for both sides. The move it plays will be a result of each side trying to maximise their own score and minimising their opponent's score. Hence the term *minimax* search.

The quality of the move chosen will depend on how good the *evaluation* is and how deep the *search* is.

The positions searched form the shape of a *tree*. The game position is called the *root*. Moves generated from the root and other moves are called branches and at the end of branches are leaves. Positions searched are called *nodes*. Hence we get the term *search tree*.

Coding style

I have aimed to make the code as simple as possible, while aiming to make the engine run fast. Speed is a priority over memory usage.

You do not need to be an expert programmer to follow the code. Some programming features include:

- The program makes extensive use of bitboards and bitwise operations.
- The program makes extensive use of arrays to create tables.
- Function parameters are declared with the **const** keyword wherever possible. I have found that this makes passing arguments faster than passing by reference.
- Integers are used instead of floating point numbers wherever possible.
- **#define** values are in uppercase.
- Normally I use indentation of 4 spaces, however, here it is only 2 spaces. This is to reduce lines of code wrapping over 2 lines.

Arrays

Chess engines make extensive use of arrays. An array is a way a computer program stores a number of *like* items. For example, the 64 squares of a chessboard can be represented by an array of 64 elements, one representing each square. Arrays start with an index number of zero, so the first square (A1 In algebraic notation) would have an index of zero, while the last square (H8) has an index number of 63.

FM Bill Jordan

What is a Bitboard?

```
#define U64 unsigned __int64
```

A U64 is an unsigned long integer. It contains 64 bits. This is very useful for chess programs because there are 64 squares on a chessboard. A bitboard is simply a 64 bit integer. The beauty of this is that each bit can represent one square of a chessboard. Bitboards are also called *bitmaps* or *bitplanes*.

In computer memory a bitboard with a value of zero would be a sequence of 64 zeroes that would look like this.

0000000000000000000000000000000000000000000000000000000000000000

It can be thought of a binary number, in which any digit could be a 0 or 1.

1111111111111111111111111111111111111111111111111111111111111111

This is the largest possible number, which is 2 to the power of 64.

A bitboard may have a single positive bit. These bitboards always have a value of 2 to the power of something.

It can be presented as an 8x8 grid. For us humans it is easier for us to visualise it like this.

```
0 0 0 0 0 0 0 0
0 0 0 0 0 0 0 0
0 0 0 0 0 0 0 0
0 0 0 0 0 0 0 0
0 0 0 0 0 0 0 0
0 0 0 0 0 0 0 0
0 0 0 0 0 0 0 0
0 0 0 0 0 0 0 0
```

```
A1 B1 C1 D1 E1 F1 G1 H1
A2 B2 C2 D2 E2 F2 G2 H2
A3 B3 C3 D3 E3 F3 G3 H3
A4 B4 C4 D4 E4 F4 G4 H4
A5 B5 C5 D5 E5 F5 G5 H5
A6 B6 C6 D6 E6 F6 G6 H6
A7 B7 C7 D7 E7 F7 G7 H7
A8 B8 C8 D8 E8 F8 G8 H8
```

Note that the top right corner is A1 in Algebraic notation. Some engines have A8 in the top left corner. However, as a chess player, I prefer the zero square being A1. However, to make boards easier to visualise, bitboard diagrams in this book have white at the bottom.

Important Bitboards

U64 bit_pieces[2][6]

This is an array of bitboards representing the position of the 12 types of chess units. It is used extensively in the program.

- **bit_pieces[White][P]** represents white pawns.
- **bit_pieces[White][N]** represents white knights.
- **bit_pieces[White][B]** represents white bishops.
- **bit_pieces[White][R]** represents white rooks.
- **bit_pieces[White][Q]** represents white queens.
- **bit_pieces[White][K]** represents the white king.

bit_pieces[Black][P] represents black pawns etc.

The following bitboards are related to the initial position.

```
0 0 0 0 0 0 0 0
0 0 0 0 0 0 0 0
0 0 0 0 0 0 0 0
0 0 0 0 0 0 0 0
0 0 0 0 0 0 0 0
0 0 0 0 0 0 0 0
1 1 1 1 1 1 1 1
0 0 0 0 0 0 0 0
```
white pawns

```
0 0 0 0 0 0 0 0
0 0 0 0 0 0 0 0
0 0 0 0 0 0 0 0
0 0 0 0 0 0 0 0
0 0 0 0 0 0 0 0
0 0 0 0 0 0 0 0
0 0 0 0 0 0 0 0
0 1 0 0 0 0 1 0
```
white knights

```
0 0 0 0 0 0 0 0
0 0 0 0 0 0 0 0
0 0 0 0 0 0 0 0
0 0 0 0 0 0 0 0
0 0 0 0 0 0 0 0
0 0 0 0 0 0 0 0
0 0 0 0 0 0 0 0
0 0 1 0 0 1 0 0
```
white bishops

```
0 0 0 0 0 0 0 0
0 0 0 0 0 0 0 0
0 0 0 0 0 0 0 0
0 0 0 0 0 0 0 0
0 0 0 0 0 0 0 0
0 0 0 0 0 0 0 0
0 0 0 0 0 0 0 0
1 0 0 0 0 0 0 1
```
white rooks

```
0 0 0 0 0 0 0 0
0 0 0 0 0 0 0 0
0 0 0 0 0 0 0 0
0 0 0 0 0 0 0 0
0 0 0 0 0 0 0 0
0 0 0 0 0 0 0 0
0 0 0 0 0 0 0 0
0 0 0 1 0 0 0 0
```
white queens

```
0 0 0 0 0 0 0 0
0 0 0 0 0 0 0 0
0 0 0 0 0 0 0 0
0 0 0 0 0 0 0 0
0 0 0 0 0 0 0 0
0 0 0 0 0 0 0 0
0 0 0 0 0 0 0 0
0 0 0 0 1 0 0 0
```
white king

U64 bit_units[2]

Each element of the array represents the units of one side.

```
0 0 0 0 0 0 0 0
0 0 0 0 0 0 0 0
0 0 0 0 0 0 0 0
0 0 0 0 0 0 0 0
0 0 0 0 0 0 0 0
0 0 0 0 0 0 0 0
1 1 1 1 1 1 1 1
1 1 1 1 1 1 1 1
```

This bitboard **bit_units[White]** represents the white units in the initial position.

U64 bit_all

This is a bitboard representing all the occupied squares on the board.

```
1 1 1 1 1 1 1 1
1 1 1 1 1 1 1 1
0 0 0 0 0 0 0 0
0 0 0 0 0 0 0 0
0 0 0 0 0 0 0 0
0 0 0 0 0 0 0 0
1 1 1 1 1 1 1 1
1 1 1 1 1 1 1 1
```

bit_all in the initial position looks like this.

U64 bit_between[64][64]

bit_between represents the squares between two different squares on the same line. If the squares are not on the same rank, file or diagonal then the value is always zero. If the squares are adjacent then the value is always zero. It can be used with **bit_all** to see whether a line is blocked. The values are prefilled when the program first starts.

U64 bit_after[64][64]

This relates to the squares **after** the second square on a line. **bit_after** stores the inverse of these squares.

Bitboards and Functions

Sometimes it is useful to pass bitboards to functions.

Bitboards may be declared as local variables. For example **BITBOARD b1, b2** creates two temporary bitboards.

Bitwise Operations

Bitwise operations can be used with *bitboards*. With bitboards, you can do all kinds of tricks.

- The bitwise operator OR | can be used to combine 2 bitboards.
- The bitwise operator AND **&** can be used to find which bits

are in common with 2 bitboards.
- The bitwise operator XOR ^ can be used to find what bits in two bitboards are mutually exclusive.
- The bitwise operator NOT ~ can be used to a reverse a bitboard.
- The bitwise operators LEFT SHIFT << and RIGHT SHIFT >> can be used to shift all the bits in a bitboard.

Bitwise OR

bit_all = bit_units[White] | bit_units[Black]
bit_all is now bit_units[White] and bit_units[Black] combined.
bit_all contains 32 bits, while bit_units[White] and
bit_units[Black] contain 16 bits each.

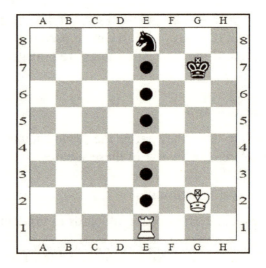

Bitwise AND

Can the rook on e1 capture the knight on e8?

```
0 0 0 0 0 0 0 0
0 0 0 0 1 0 0 0
0 0 0 0 1 0 0 0
0 0 0 0 1 0 0 0
0 0 0 0 1 0 0 0
0 0 0 0 1 0 0 0
```

```
0 0 0 0 1 0 0 0
0 0 0 0 0 0 0 0
```

This is a bitboard representing **between[E1][E8]**

```
0 0 0 0 1 0 0 0
0 0 0 0 0 0 1 0
0 0 0 0 0 0 0 0
0 0 0 0 0 0 0 0
0 0 0 0 0 0 0 0
0 0 0 0 0 0 0 0
0 0 0 0 0 0 1 0
0 0 0 0 1 0 0 0
```

This is a bitboard representing **bit_all**

We want to look at the squares between e1 and e8. We use **between[E1][E8]**. We check the result of **bit_between[E1][E8] & bit_all**. The result is zero so it means nothing is blocking the rook.

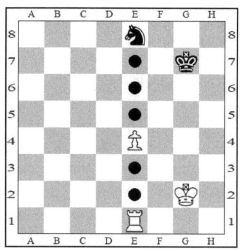

This time the pawn on e4 is blocking the rook, so **between[E1] [E8] & bit_all** is nonzero, so the rook is blocked.

Note that **between[E1][E8]** and **between[E8][E1]** have the same value. It doesn't matter what order the squares are in.

Bitwise NOT

~ inverts the bits.

```
1 1 1 1 1 1 1 1
1 1 1 1 1 1 1 1
0 0 0 0 0 0 0 0
0 0 0 0 0 0 0 0
0 0 0 0 0 0 0 0
0 0 0 0 0 0 0 0
1 1 1 1 1 1 1 1
1 1 1 1 1 1 1 1
```

This represents the pieces in the initial position with **bit_all**.

```
0 0 0 0 0 0 0 0
0 0 0 0 0 0 0 0
1 1 1 1 1 1 1 1
1 1 1 1 1 1 1 1
1 1 1 1 1 1 1 1
1 1 1 1 1 1 1 1
0 0 0 0 0 0 0 0
0 0 0 0 0 0 0 0
```

This is the inverse **~bit_all**.

Bitwise XOR

This is the mutually exclusive operation on the bits. It might not be useful with occupied squares, but could be useful with attacked squares.

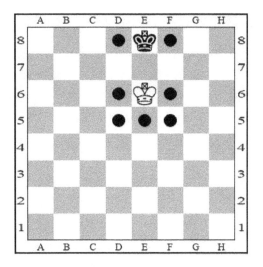

```
0 0 0 1 0 1 0 0
0 0 0 0 0 0 0 0
0 0 0 1 0 1 0 0
0 0 0 1 1 1 0 0
0 0 0 0 0 0 0 0
0 0 0 0 0 0 0 0
0 0 0 0 0 0 0 0
0 0 0 0 0 0 0 0
```

For example, this is the bitboard of **bit_moves[K][E6] ^ bit_moves[K][E8]**. **bit_moves[K][64]** is prefilled with possible king moves from each square.

Bitwise SHIFT LEFT and SHIFT RIGHT

The bitwise left operator shifts all bits in a bitboard to the left. The value of a shift can be any positive number within 1 up to the size of the array.

For example, here is a bitboard **b1** for a single bit, representing a King on E2. White is at the bottom of the board.

21

```
0 0 0 0 0 0 0 0
0 0 0 0 0 0 0 0
0 0 0 0 0 0 0 0
0 0 0 0 0 0 0 0
0 0 0 0 0 0 0 0
0 0 0 0 0 0 0 0
0 0 0 0 1 0 0 0
0 0 0 0 0 0 0 0
```

```
BITBOARD b1 = bit_pieces[White][K];
```

- b1 >> 1 would move the King one square to the right, i.e. **f2**.
- b1 << 1 would move the King one square to the left, i.e. **d2**.
- b1 >> 7 would move the King one square up and to the left, i.e., **d3**.
- b1 >> 8 would move the King one square up, i.e. **e3**.
- b1 >> 9 would move the King one square up and to the right, i.e., **f3**.
- b1 << 7 would move the King one square down and to the left, i.e., **d1**.
- b1 << 8 would move the King one square down, i.e. **e1**.
- b1 << 9 would move the King one square down and to the right, i.e., **f1**.

Larger numbers may shift bits more squares. For example, **b1 >> 56** would move the King all the way from **e1** to **e8**. Note that if a bit is shifted off the board, it vanishes. For example, **b1 >> 64** results in zero.

Bitboards with multiple bits are shifted in the same way. In some cases, some bits are lost while others are moved, but remain on the board.

The bitwise shift operators can be especially useful for pawns. For example, **b1 = bit_pieces[White][P] >> 8 & bit_all** would result in zero if all the white pawns are blocked.

Bitwise NOT

The ! is not a bitwise operator; it is a logical operator. The ~ is the bitwise NOT operator. It flips every bit in a bitboard.

Looping through Bitboards

There are many times this program loops through bitboards.

```
while(b1)
{
  sq = NextBit(b1);
  //do something with sq.
  b1 &= b1 - 1;
}
```

Example:
sq = NextBit(b1);
This converts the next bit in the bitboard **b1** to a square, which has a value between 0 and 63 inclusive.

b1 &= b1 - 1; removes one bit from the bitboard. This bit is the bit representing **sq**. The bitboard has one bit less each time through the loop. When the bitboard is reduced to zero, then the **while loop** finishes.

b1 &= not_mask[i] is equivalent to **b1 &=~mask[i]**. Because ~**mask[i]** is apparently a little slow, **not_mask** pre-calculates the values and stores them in an array. However, **b1 &= b1 1;** is even faster.

Source Files

globals.h contains elements that are used in more than one source file. These include:

- Variables
- Arrays
- Structures
- Function prototypes

gen.cpp is to do with move move generation. All legal moves are generated from the current position, including captures, castling, pawn promotion and *en passant* captures.

attack.cpp contains functions that determine if a square is attacked by a given side and the lowest attacker of a square.

bitboard.cpp contains functions and data structures which process bitboards.

update.cpp deals with updating information whenever a move is made or unmade.

init.cpp contains functions that run before a game starts.

search.cpp contains the main search loop.

eval.cpp deals with evaluation.

hash.cpp contains functions handling the hash tables.

main.cpp contains functions for connecting to Winboard.

globals.h

```
#include  < memory.h >
#include  < conio.h >
#include  < stdio.h >
#include  < stdlib.h >
#include  < math.h >
#include  < string.h >
#include  < dos.h >
#include  < time.h >
```

/* These include standard libraries from which some functions are used. For example, **memory.h** includes the **memset** function. */

```
#define U64 unsigned __int64
#define BITBOARD unsigned __int64
```

/* U64 and BITBOARD are both 64-bit integers, but having different names may help explain the context. */

```
enum{
A1, B1, C1, D1, E1, F1, G1, H1,
A2, B2, C2, D2, E2, F2, G2, H2,
A3, B3, C3, D3, E3, F3, G3, H3,
A4, B4, C4, D4, E4, F4, G4, H4,
A5, B5, C5, D5, E5, F5, G5, H5,
A6, B6, C6, D6, E6, F6, G6, H6,
A7, B7, C7, D7, E7, F7, G7, H7,
A8, B8, C8, D8, E8, F8, G8, H8
};
```

/* The 64 squares of the chessboard are defined with their algebraic names. A1 is 0, H8 is 63, etc. Some of these squares are used in the code for castling. They are very useful for debugging. */

```
#define NORTH 0
#define NE 1
#define EAST 2
#define SE 3
#define SOUTH 4
```

```
#define SW 5
#define WEST 6
#define NW 7
```

/* These represent different directions the line pieces can move in. They are from White's point of view, with **NORTH** being up the board. They are used in move generation. */

```
#define P 0
#define N 1
#define B 2
#define R 3
#define Q 4
#define K 5
#define EMPTY 6
```

/* The 6 pieces are represented by their initial letter. N is used instead of K to distinguish Knight from King. */

```
#define White 0
#define Black 1
```

/* Colours are represented by **White** and **Black**. I was unable to use WHITE and BLACK, which couldn't be used because they were reserved by Visual C++. */

```
#define MAX_PLY 64
#define MOVE_STACK 4000
```

/* This is the maximum size for the total number of moves in **move_list**. At an average of about 40 legal moves in a position, this is enough for a depth of about 50 ply. 2000 should be more than enough; however, if this is exceeded by a deep search, consider increasing it. */

```
game game_list[GAME_STACK];
```

/* Moves for the entire game are stored in an array of type move called **game_list**. **game_list** is used with **hply** to store information about a move played so the move can be taken back. */

```
#define GAME_STACK 2000
```

/* This is the max size for the total number of moves in **game_list** including moves being searched. At an average of about 40 legal moves in a position, this is enough for a depth of about 50 ply. */

```
#define HASH_SCORE   100000000
```

/* HASH_SCORE is added to the move score so that the move from the hash table is searched first. */

```
#define CAPTURE_SCORE 10000000
```

/* CAPTURE_SCORE is added to the move score so that captures are searched after the move from the hash table. */

```
typedef struct {
  int from;
  int to;
  unsigned int flags;
  int score;
  } move_data;
```

/* The **move** structure stores information about a move.

- **from** is the start square.
- **to** is the destination square.
- **flags** contains information for special moves.
- **score** is used when sorting moves. Moves with higher scores will be searched first.

*/

```
typedef struct {
  int from;
  int to;
  unsigned int flags;
  int capture;
  int fifty;
  int castle;
  BITBOARD hash;
  BITBOARD lock;
```

```
} game_data;
```

/* The **game** structure is similar to the move structure. **from, to** and **flags** are the same, however there is no **score**.

- **fifty** keeps track of how many moves since the last pawn move or capture.
- **capture** is the type of captured piece, if any.
- **castle** stores castle permissions.
- **hash** stores a number to help test for repetition.
- **lock** also stores a number to help test for repetition.

Included in globals.h are prototypes for functions that are used in more than one source file.

For example, **bool Attack(const int s,const int sq);** allows the function **Attack** to be used in any file that includes **globals.h**.

Also included in globals.h are global variables, arrays and structures.

For example, **extern int nodes;** allows the variable **nodes** to be used in any file that includes **globals.h**. */

bitboard.cpp

```
#include "globals.h"
BITBOARD bit_pawncaptures[2][64];
BITBOARD bit_left[2][64];
BITBOARD bit_right[2][64];
```

/* These store bitboards for pawn captures, for each side. */

```
BITBOARD bit_moves[6][64];
```

/* **bit_moves[]** store 64 bitboards for each square, each type of piece can move to. */

```
BITBOARD bit_pieces[2][7];
BITBOARD bit_units[2];
BITBOARD bit_all;
```

/* These bitboards are used with move generation. */

```
BITBOARD bit_between[64][64];
BITBOARD bit_after[64][64];
```

/* These bitboards are used with move generation. */

```
BITBOARD mask_passed[2][64];
BITBOARD mask_path[2][64];
```

/* These bitboards are used with passed pawns. */

```
BITBOARD mask[64];
BITBOARD not_mask[64];
```

/* **mask[]** stores single bit bitboards for each square. **not_mask[]** is the opposite of **mask[]**. It contains every other square. */
BITBOARD mask_cols[64];

/* **mask_cols[]** is used to detect open and half-open files. */

```
BITBOARD mask_isolated[64];
```

/* This array is used to detect isolated pawns. An isolated pawn is a pawn that cannot be defended by another pawn. */

```
BITBOARD mask_kingside;
BITBOARD mask_queenside;
```

/* The queenside is the A, B, C and D files, while the kingside is the E, F, G and H files. */

```
BITBOARD not_a_file;
BITBOARD not_h_file;
```

/* These may be used to detect if a square is on one of the rook files. */

```
int pawnplus[2][64];
int pawndouble[2][64];
int pawnleft[2][64];
int pawnright[2][64];
```

/* These arrays are used with pawn moves and captures. */

```
void SetRanks();
void SetRowCol();
void SetBetweenVector();
static int GetEdge(int sq, int plus);
```

/* **GetEdge()** calculates the last square in a rank, file or diagonal. It is used by **SetBitAfter()**. */

```
void SetBit(BITBOARD& bb, int square);
void SetBitFalse(BITBOARD& bb, int square);
```

/* These set single bits. */

```
int NextBit(BITBOARD bb);
```

/* This finds the next bit in a bitboard. */

```
void PrintBitBoard(BITBOARD bb);
void PrintCell(int x, BITBOARD bb);
```

/* These may be used in debugging. */

```
Function prototypes are here.
void SetBit(BITBOARD& bb, int square)
{
  bb |= (1ui64 <  <  square);
}
```

/* This sets a bit of a corresponding square to 1.

```
0 0 0 0 0 0 0 0
0 0 0 0 0 0 0 0
0 0 0 0 0 0 0 0
0 0 0 0 0 0 0 0
0 0 0 0 0 0 0 0
0 0 0 0 0 0 0 0
0 0 0 0 0 0 0 0
0 0 0 0 1 0 0 0
```

U64 b1 = 0;
This creates an empty bitboard. This is the bitboard after
SetBit(E1); */

```
void SetBitFalse(BITBOARD& bb, int square)
{
  bb &= ~mask[square];
}
```

/* This sets a bit of a corresponding square to 0.

SetBits()

SetBits() is called before the game starts. It prefills numerous arrays of bitboards and other structures. These can later be used as *Look up tables* which help the engine run faster. */

31

```
void SetBits()
{
  memset(bit_pawncaptures, 0,
sizeof(bit_pawncaptures));
  memset(bit_moves, 0, sizeof(bit_moves));
  SetRanks();
  SetMasks();
  SetPawnArrays();
  SetPawnBits();
  SetPassedBits();
  SetBetweenVector();
  SetBitAfter();
}
```

SetRanks()

/* **SetRanks()** sets the rank from each player's end of the board. For example, the squares A1-H1 are white's rank[0][0] while they are black's rank[1][7]. */

```
static void SetRanks()
{
  for (int x = 0; x < 64; x++)
  {
    rank[White][x] = row[x];
    rank[Black][x] = 7 - row[x];
  }
}
```

SetMasks()

/* **SetMasks()** prefills various masks. */

```
static void SetMasks()
{
  for (int x = 0; x < 64; x++)
  {
    SetBit(mask[x], x);
    not_mask[x] = ~mask[x];
  }
  for (int x = 0; x < 64; x++)
  {
    if (col[x] < 2)
      SetBit(mask_queenside, x);
    if (col[x] > 5)
```

```
        SetBit(mask_kingside, x);
  }
  for (int x = 0; x < 64; x++)
    for (int y = 0; y < 64; y++)
    {
      if (col[x] == col[y])
        SetBit(mask_cols[x], y);
    }
  not_a_file = ~mask_cols[0];
  not_h_file = ~mask_cols[7];
}
```

/* **mask_queenside** and **mask_kingside** are used to help evaluate pawn cover for the kings in the middlegame.

SetPawnArrays()

SetPawnArrays() prefill arrays that store potential pawn captures and moves. */

```
static void SetPawnArrays()
{
  for (int x = 0; x < 64; x++)
  {
    pawnleft[0][x] = -1;
    pawnleft[1][x] = -1;
    pawnright[0][x] = -1;
    pawnright[1][x] = -1;
    if (col[x] > 0)
    {
      if (row[x] < 7) { pawnleft[0][x] = x + 7; }
      if (row[x] > 0) { pawnleft[1][x] = x - 9; }
    }
    if (col[x] < 7)
    {
      if (row[x] < 7) { pawnright[0][x] = x + 9; }
      if (row[x] > 0) { pawnright[1][x] = x - 7; }
    }
    if (row[x] < 7)
      pawnplus[0][x] = x + 8;
    if (row[x] < 6)
      pawndouble[0][x] = x + 16;
    if (row[x] > 0)
      pawnplus[1][x] = x - 8;
    if (row[x] > 1)
```

```
        pawndouble[1][x] = x - 16;
    }
}
```

SetPawnBits()

/* **SetPawnBits()** sets the masks for pawn captures. */

```
static void SetPawnBits()
{
  for (int x = 0; x < 64; x++)
  {
    if (col[x] > 0)
    {
      if (row[x] < 7)
      {
        SetBit(bit_pawncaptures[0][x], pawnleft[0]
[x]);
        SetBit(bit_left[0][x], pawnleft[0][x]);
      }
      if (row[x] > 0)
      {
        SetBit(bit_pawncaptures[1][x], pawnleft[1]
[x]);
        SetBit(bit_left[1][x], pawnleft[1][x]);
      }
    }
    if (col[x] < 7)
    {
      if (row[x] < 7)
      {
        SetBit(bit_pawncaptures[0][x], pawnright[0]
[x]);
        SetBit(bit_right[0][x], pawnright[0][x]);
      }
      if (row[x] > 0)
      {
        SetBit(bit_pawncaptures[1][x], pawnright[1]
[x]);
        SetBit(bit_right[1][x], pawnright[1][x]);
      }
    }
  }
}
```

SetPassedBits()

/* **SetPassedBits()** sets the masks for isolated pawns, passed pawns and paths of pawns. */

```
static void SetPassedBits()
{
  for (int x = 0; x < 64; x++)
    for (int y = 0; y < 64; y++)
    {
      if (abs(col[x] - col[y]) < 2)
      {
        if (row[x] < row[y] && row[y] < 7)
          SetBit(mask_passed[White][x], y);
        if (row[x] > row[y] && row[y] > 0)
          SetBit(mask_passed[Black][x], y);
      }
      if (abs(col[x] - col[y]) == 1)
      {
        SetBit(mask_isolated[x], y);
      }
      if (col[x] == col[y])
      {
        if (row[x] < row[y])
          SetBit(mask_path[White][x], y);
        if (row[x] > row[y])
          SetBit(mask_path[Black][x], y);
      }
    }
}
```

SetBetweenVector()

/* **bit_between** is a vector that represents the squares between one square and another. If the 2 squares not on the same rank, file or diagonal or are adjacent , then **bit_between** will have a value of zero. It is used to detect whether any units are between the two squares or not. */

```
static void SetBetweenVector()
{
  int x, y, z;
  for (x = 0; x < 64; x++)
    for (y = 0; y < 64; y++)
    {
```

```
      if (row[x] == row[y])
      {
        if (y > x)
          for (z = x + 1; z < y; z++)
            SetBit(bit_between[x][y], z);
        else
          for (z = y + 1; z < x;  z++)
            SetBit(bit_between[x][y], z);
      }
      if (col[x] == col[y])
      {
        if (y > x)
          for (z = x + 8; z < y; z += 8)
            SetBit(bit_between[x][y], z);
        else
          for (z = y + 8; z < x; z += 8)
            SetBit(bit_between[x][y], z);
      }
      if (nwdiag[x] == nwdiag[y])
      {
        if (y > x)
          for (z = x + 7; z < y; z += 7)
            SetBit(bit_between[x][y], z);
        else
          for (z = y + 7; z < x; z += 7)
            SetBit(bit_between[x][y], z);
      }
      if (nediag[x] == nediag[y])
      {
        if (y > x)
          for (z = x + 9; z < y; z += 9)
            SetBit(bit_between[x][y], z);
        else
          for (z = y + 9; z < x; z += 9)
            SetBit(bit_between[x][y], z);
      }
    }
  }
}
```

SetBitAfter()

/* **bit_after** is a vector, representing the squares on the same line, **after** two other squares. It is used in move and capture generation of bishops, rooks and queens. */

```
static void SetBitAfter()
```

```
{
  int x, y, z;
  for (x = 0; x < 64; x++)
    for (y = 0; y < 64; y++)
    {
      if (x == y)
        continue;
      if (row[x] == row[y])
      {
        if (y > x)
          for (z = y; z <= row[y] * 8 + 7; z++)
            SetBit(bit_after[x][y], z);
        else
          for (z = y; z >= row[y] * 8; z--)
            SetBit(bit_after[x][y], z);
      }
      if (col[x] == col[y])
      {
        if (y > x)
          for (z = y; z <= 56 + col[y]; z += 8)
            SetBit(bit_after[x][y], z);
        else
          for (z = y; z >= col[y]; z -= 8)
            SetBit(bit_after[x][y], z);
      }
      if (nwdiag[x] == nwdiag[y])
      {
        if (y > x)
          for (z = y; z <= GetEdge(x, 7); z += 7)
            SetBit(bit_after[x][y], z);
        else
          for (z = y; z >= GetEdge(x, -7); z -= 7)
            SetBit(bit_after[x][y], z);
      }
      if (nediag[x] == nediag[y])
      {
        if (y > x)
          for (int z = y; z <= GetEdge(x, 9); z += 9)
            SetBit(bit_after[x][y], z);
        else
          for (int z = y; z >= GetEdge(x, -9); z -= 9)
            SetBit(bit_after[x][y], z);
      }
    }
  for (int x = 0; x < 64; x++)
    for (int y = 0; y < 64; y++)
    {
```

```
        bit_after[x][y] = ~bit_after[x][y];
    }
}
```

/* Here is an example of **bit_between**.

```
0 0 0 0 0 0 0 0
0 0 0 0 0 0 0 0
0 0 0 0 0 0 0 0
0 0 0 0 0 0 0 0
0 1 1 1 1 1 1 0
0 0 0 0 0 0 0 0
0 0 0 0 0 0 0 0
0 0 0 0 0 0 0 0
```

This is the bitboard of **bit_between[A4][H4]**. It can be used to test if there is a piece between a4 and h4.

bit_after is similar to **bit_between**, except that **bit_after** is composed of the bits from and including the second array element.

```
0 0 0 0 0 0 0 0
0 0 0 0 0 0 0 0
0 0 0 0 0 0 0 0
0 0 0 0 0 0 0 0
0 0 0 0 1 1 1 1
0 0 0 0 0 0 0 0
0 0 0 0 0 0 0 0
0 0 0 0 0 0 0 0
```

This is the bitboard of **bit_after[A4][E4]**. A4 and E4 set the direction of the vector. In this case, it is left to right.

bit_after[A4][E4] consists of the bit representing E4 and the squares that follow, which are F4, G4 and H4. **bit_after** can be used in move generation.

GetEdge()

GetEdge returns the edge square when moving in a certain

38

direction. */

```
static int GetEdge(int sq, int plus)
{
  do
  {
    sq += plus;
  } while (col[sq] > 0 && col[sq] < 7 && row[sq] > 0
&& row[sq] < 7);
  return sq;
}
```

/* There are 8 possible directions from a square.

- Plus one square right.
- Minus one square left.
- Plus 8 squares up.
- Minus 8 squares down.
- Plus 7 squares up and left.
- Minus 9 squares down and left.
- Plus 9 squares up and right.
- Minus 7 squares down and right.

GetEdge is used to help prefill **bit_after**.

The following table is used with **NextBit()**. */

```
const int lsb_64_table[64] =
{
   63, 30,  3, 32, 59, 14, 11, 33,
   60, 24, 50,  9, 55, 19, 21, 34,
   61, 29,  2, 53, 51, 23, 41, 18,
   56, 28,  1, 43, 46, 27,  0, 35,
   62, 31, 58,  4,  5, 49, 54,  6,
   15, 52, 12, 40,  7, 42, 45, 16,
   25, 57, 48, 13, 10, 39,  8, 44,
   20, 47, 38, 22, 17, 37, 36, 26
};
int NextBit(BITBOARD bb)
{
    unsigned int folded;
    bb ^= bb - 1;
    folded = (int) bb ^ (bb  >>  32);
```

```
    return lsb_64_table[folded * 0x78291ACF  >>  26];
}
```

/* The above is Matt's folding trick, which I found on the excellent website chessprogramming.org. It's 32-bit friendly so it can work with 32-bit operating systems.

PrintBitBoard() is a very useful function. It receives a bitboard as an argument and returns a number from 0-63 representing a square. There are faster functions that only work on 64-bit operating systems. */

```
void PrintBitBoard(BITBOARD bb)
{
  printf("\n");
  int x;
  for (x = 56; x < 64; x++)
    PrintCell(x, bb);
  for (x = 48; x < 56; x++)
    PrintCell(x, bb);
  for (x = 40; x < 48; x++)
    PrintCell(x, bb);
  for (x = 32; x < 40; x++)
    PrintCell(x, bb);
  for (x = 24; x < 32; x++)
    PrintCell(x, bb);
  for (x = 16; x < 24; x++)
    PrintCell(x, bb);
  for (x = 8; x < 16; x++)
    PrintCell(x, bb);
  for (x = 0; x < 8; x++)
    PrintCell(x, bb);
}
```

/* This can be used to display a bitboard for debugging purposes. */

```
void PrintCell(int x, BITBOARD bb)
{
  if (mask[x] & bb)
    printf(" X");
  else
    printf(" -");
  if ((x + 1) % 8 == 0)printf("\n");
```

}

/* This is used with **PrintBitBoard()**.

Other Bitboards

- As well as detecting passed and isolated pawns, bitboards can be used for recognising all sorts of pawn structures.
- The square of the pawn, which is used to see if a king can catch a passed pawn.
- Detecting checks.
- Detecting pinned pieces.
- Detecting attack and defence patterns, etc.

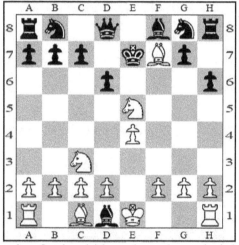

This is an example of using bitboards to detect knight checks. For example, **bit_knight_moves[c3] & bit_knight_moves[bit_pieces[B][K]** returns **d5**, while **bit_knight_moves[E5] & bit_knight_moves[bit_pieces[1][K]]** returns **c6** and **g6**.

Tables

There are many tables in a chess program. Most are integer arrays of size 64 to represent the 64 squares of the board. /* **not_a_file** and **not_h_file** can be used to see whether a piece or pawn is on a rook file. */

init.cpp

```
int side;
```

/* represents the side to move. It's either 0 (White) or 1 (Black). */

```
int xside;
```

/* **xside** represents the other side. The use of **xside** was a convention in the public domain *GNUChess* engine. **s** and **xs** can also represent the side and other side. */

```
s ^ 1;
```

/* If **s** is 0 then **s^1** is 1. If **s** is 1 then **s^1** is 0. Sometimes you only know one side, and it is good to know the other side. */

```
side ^= 1;
```

/* changes the value of **side** from 0 to 1 and vice versa. */

```
int fifty;
```

/* Keeps track of how many moves have been played since the last pawn move or capture. When 100 ply without a pawn move or capture has been reached, it is a draw by the 50 move rule.

It is also used to detect repetition. To detect repetition, you search through the previous moves (both played and searched) till the last pawn move or capture, to see if the position has been repeated. */

```
int nodes;
```

/* A **node** is a position in the search tree that is searched. **nodes** is the total number of nodes searched since the start of a turn. A **ply** is one half-move, either by white or black. 2 ply is a move by both sides, what in chess is called a move. A **depth** of 5 plies means looking ahead 5 plies. */

```
int ply;
```

/* For simplicity and because it is used frequently, **ply** is a global variable. Global variables are sometimes frowned upon in programming, however, in this program it makes things simpler in some ways. */

```
#define MAX_PLY 64
```

/* This is the maximum possible ply. If this limit is exceeded in some searches, consider increasing MAX_PLY. */

```
int hply;
```

/* Keeps track of how many ply have been played since the start of the game. This allows moves to be taken back during the search. */

```
int board[64];
```

/* Represents the board.

Squares range from 0 - 63 inclusive. 0 is **A1** in Algebraic notation while 63 is **H8**. Some programs do it in the opposite direction, which, as a chess player, I found very confusing. */

History Tables

```
int history[64][64];
```

/* The history table helps to improve move order. The more often a move has caused a **beta-cutoff**, the more likely the same move will cause a cutoff in a different position.

This table is cleared at the start of the turn.

Every time a non-capturing move causes a **beta cutoff**, the from and to squares of the move are stored in the history table. In most cases, a move that matches a history move involved the same type of piece. There are some exceptions:

- A queen move may match with a rook or bishop move and vice versa.
- A king move could match a move by any other piece except a knight.
- A pawn could match a move by any other piece except a knight or bishop.

These incorrect matches make history tables slightly less efficient. However, they do not happen often.

History tables match a move better if the same type of piece moves as in the original move.

Capturing moves are not included because:

- Captures that caused a cutoff are likely to have done so because they are captures. It makes no sense to match them with non-captures.
- Captures have their own sorting algorithm, which is better than using history moves.

When a move is added to the move list during move generation, non-capturing moves are given the history score. Moves with a higher history score will be searched first. */

```
int square_score[2][6][64];
```

/* **square_score[]** stores values of pieces for each square. These remain the same for the entire game, except for the king, which has a different table for the endgame. */

```
int king_endgame[2][64];
```

/* **king_endgame[]** stores values of the king position in the endgame for each square. */

Material

```
int pawn_mat[2];
```

/* **pawn_mat[]** stores total pawn values for both sides, in centipawns. */

```
int piece_mat[2];
```

/* **piece_mat[]** stores total piece values for both sides, but does not include pawns. */

Passed Pawns

```
int passed[2][64];
```

/* **passed[]** stores values of passed pawns for both sides on any square of the board.

Note that there is no score for pawns on the seventh rank, as any pawns there are always passed, so the score is built into the square score table. */

Move Lists

```
move move_list[MOVE_STACK];
```

/* Moves are stored in an array of type move called **move_list**. Only nodes in the current variation have their move list stored. There are move lists for each ply. */

```
first_move[MAX_PLY];
```

/* This stores the starting point for the move lists of each ply.

The move list for ply 1 starts at 0 and ends just before **first_move[1]**.
The move list for ply 2 starts at **first_move[1]** and ends just before **first_move[2]**.
The move list for ply 3 starts at **first_move[2]** and ends just before **first_move[3]**.
etc. so the move list for any ply is between **first_move[ply]** and **first_move[ply + 1]**. */

```
const char piece_char[6] =
{
  'P', 'N', 'B', 'R', 'Q', 'K'
};
```

/* These are the initial letters of each piece. They are used when displaying moves. */

```
const int piece_value[6] =
{
  100, 300, 300, 500, 900, 10000
};
```

/* These are the values of each type of piece in *centipawns*. A centipawn is a hundredth of a pawn.

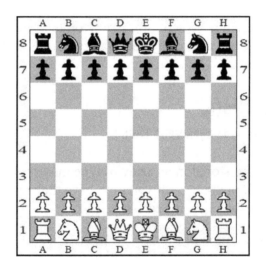

*/

```
const int init_color[64] =
{
  0, 0, 0, 0, 0, 0, 0, 0,
  0, 0, 0, 0, 0, 0, 0, 0,
  6, 6, 6, 6, 6, 6, 6, 6,
  6, 6, 6, 6, 6, 6, 6, 6,
  6, 6, 6, 6, 6, 6, 6, 6,
  6, 6, 6, 6, 6, 6, 6, 6,
  1, 1, 1, 1, 1, 1, 1, 1,
  1, 1, 1, 1, 1, 1, 1, 1
```

`};`

/* **init_color[64]** is initialised with the starting color for each
square (0 = White, 1 = Black, 6 = EMPTY). */

```
const int init_piece[64] =
{
  3, 1, 2, 4, 5, 2, 1, 3,
  0, 0, 0, 0, 0, 0, 0, 0,
  6, 6, 6, 6, 6, 6, 6, 6,
  6, 6, 6, 6, 6, 6, 6, 6,
  6, 6, 6, 6, 6, 6, 6, 6,
  6, 6, 6, 6, 6, 6, 6, 6,
  0, 0, 0, 0, 0, 0, 0, 0,
  3, 1, 2, 4, 5, 2, 1, 3
};
```

/* **init_piece[64]** is initialised with the starting pieces for each
square (0=pawn, 1=knight, 2=bishop, 3=rook, 4=queen, 5=king,
6=EMPTY). */

```
const int col[64]=
{
  0, 1, 2, 3, 4, 5, 6, 7,
  0, 1, 2, 3, 4, 5, 6, 7,
  0, 1, 2, 3, 4, 5, 6, 7,
  0, 1, 2, 3, 4, 5, 6, 7,
  0, 1, 2, 3, 4, 5, 6, 7,
  0, 1, 2, 3, 4, 5, 6, 7,
  0, 1, 2, 3, 4, 5, 6, 7,
  0, 1, 2, 3, 4, 5, 6, 7
};
```

/* **col** is used to determine what file a square is on.

For example, **col[H1] = 7**.

Why didn't I use the word *file*? I started coding chess engines in
BASIC in which file was a reserved word, and it became a habit
not to use *file*. */

```
const int row[64]=
{
  0, 0, 0, 0, 0, 0, 0, 0,
  1, 1, 1, 1, 1, 1, 1, 1,
  2, 2, 2, 2, 2, 2, 2, 2,
  3, 3, 3, 3, 3, 3, 3, 3,
  4, 4, 4, 4, 4, 4, 4, 4,
  5, 5, 5, 5, 5, 5, 5, 5,
  6, 6, 6, 6, 6, 6, 6, 6,
  7, 7, 7, 7, 7, 7, 7, 7
};
```

/* **row** is used to determine what rank a square is on.

For example, **row[A2] = 1**.

col and **row** values both range from 0 to 7.

This is different from real ranks and files, which range from 1 to 8.
*/

```
const int nediag[64]=
{
  14,13,12,11,10, 9, 8, 7,
  13,12,11,10, 9, 8, 7, 6,
  12,11,10, 9, 8, 7, 6, 5,
  11,10, 9, 8, 7, 6, 5, 4,
  10, 9, 8, 7, 6, 5, 4, 3,
   9, 8, 7, 6, 5, 4, 3, 2,
   8, 7, 6, 5, 4, 3, 2, 1,
   7, 6, 5, 4, 3, 2, 1, 0
};
```

/* **nediag** is used to determine what SW-NE diagonal a square is on. */

```
const int nwdiag[64]=
{
   7, 8, 9,10,11,12,13,14,
   6, 7, 8, 9,10,11,12,13,
   5, 6, 7, 8, 9,10,11,12,
   4, 5, 6, 7, 8, 9,10,11,
   3, 4, 5, 6, 7, 8, 9,10,
   2, 3, 4, 5, 6, 7, 8, 9,
```

```
    1, 2, 3, 4, 5, 6, 7, 8,
    0, 1, 2, 3, 4, 5, 6, 7
};
```

/* **nwdiag** is used to determine what SE-NW diagonal a square is
on. */

```
int Flip[64] =
{
    56,   57,   58,   59,   60,   61,   62,   63,
    48,   49,   50,   51,   52,   53,   54,   55,
    40,   41,   42,   43,   44,   45,   46,   47,
    32,   33,   34,   35,   36,   37,   38,   39,
    24,   25,   26,   27,   28,   29,   30,   31,
    16,   17,   18,   19,   20,   21,   22,   23,
    8,    9,   10,   11,   12,   13,   14,   15,
    0,    1,    2,    3,    4,    5,    6,    7
};
```

/* This is used for flipping the board. This is used to initialise
tables depending on which side of the board you are on. */

```
int pawn_score[64] =
{
    0,    0,    0,    0,    0,    0,    0,    0,
    0,    2,    4,  -12,  -12,    4,    2,    0,
    0,    2,    4,    4,    4,    4,    2,    0,
    0,    2,    4,    8,    8,    4,    2,    0,
    0,    2,    4,    8,    8,    4,    2,    0,
    4,    8,   10,   16,   16,   10,    8,    4,
  100,  100,  100,  100,  100,  100,  100,  100,
    0,    0,    0,    0,    0,    0,    0,    0
};
```

/* Note that:

- Pawns are stronger as files become more central.
- Pawns are weak on **e2** and **d2** (**e7** and **d7** for black).
- Pawns are stronger on the 6th rank.
- Pawns are very strong on the 7th rank.

Pawns are very strong on the 7th rank. They can be strong on the
6th rank because they control a lot of space. They are stronger on

more central files. Note that pawns on **e2** and **d2** have a low score to encourage the engine to move them in the opening. */

```
int knight_score[64] =
{
   -30, -20, -10,  -8,  -8, -10, -20, -30,
   -16,  -6,  -2,   0,   0,  -2,  -6, -16,
    -8,  -2,   4,   6,   6,   4,  -2,  -8,
    -5,   0,   6,   8,   8,   6,   0,  -5,
    -5,   0,   6,   8,   8,   6,   0,  -5,
   -10,  -2,   4,   6,   6,   4,  -2, -10,
   -20, -10,  -2,   0,   0,  -2, -10, -20,
  -150, -20, -10,  -5,  -5, -10, -20,-150
};
```

/* The knight gets stronger as it approaches the centre. The knight tends to be very weak in a corner on the opponent's side. It is likely to be trapped there. */

```
int bishop_score[64] =
{
   -10,  -10, -12, -10, -10, -12, -10, -10,
    0,  4,   4,   4,   4,   4,   4,   0,
    2,  4,   6,   6,   6,   6,   4,   2,
    2,  4,   6,   8,   8,   6,   4,   2,
    2,  4,   6,   8,   8,   6,   4,   2,
    2,  4,   6,   6,   6,   6,   4,   2,
   -10,  4,   4,   4,   4,   4,   4, -10,
   -10, -10, -10, -10, -10, -10, -10, -10
};
```

/* The bishop gets stronger as it approaches the centre, though it is not as weak on the edge as the knight. */

```
int rook_score[64] =
{
    4,  4,  4,  6,  6,  4,  4,  4,
    0,  0,  0,  0,  0,  0,  0,  0,
    0,  0,  0,  0,  0,  0,  0,  0,
    0,  0,  0,  0,  0,  0,  0,  0,
    0,  0,  0,  0,  0,  0,  0,  0,
    0,  0,  0,  0,  0,  0,  0,  0,
   20, 20, 20, 20, 20, 20, 20, 20,
   10, 10, 10, 10, 10, 10, 10, 10
```

```
};
```

/* The rook is stronger on the first rank, the 7th rank and the 8th rank. On the 1st and 8th ranks, it cannot be blocked by pawns. On the 7th rank it cannot be blocked by an opposing pawn defended by a pawn. A rook on the first rank tends to be stronger when on the central files. */

```
int queen_score[64] =
{
   -10, -10,  -6,  -4,  -4,  -6, -10, -10,
   -10,   2,   2,   2,   2,   2,   2, -10,
     2,   2,   2,   3,   3,   2,   2,   2,
     2,   2,   3,   4,   4,   3,   2,   2,
     2,   2,   3,   4,   4,   3,   2,   2,
     2,   2,   2,   3,   3,   2,   2,   2,
   -10,   2,   2,   2,   2,   2,   2, -10,
   -10, -10,   2,   2,   2,   2, -10, -10
};
```

/* The queen gets stronger as it approaches the centre. Squares controlled by the queen are less valuable than those controlled by a less valuable piece. */

```
int king_score[64] =
{
    20,  20,  20, -40,  10, -60,  20,  20,
    15,  20, -25, -30, -30, -45,  20,  15,
   -48, -48, -48, -48, -48, -48, -48, -48,
   -48, -48, -48, -48, -48, -48, -48, -48,
   -48, -48, -48, -48, -48, -48, -48, -48,
   -48, -48, -48, -48, -48, -48, -48, -48,
   -48, -48, -48, -48, -48, -48, -48, -48,
   -48, -48, -48, -48, -48, -48, -48, -48
};
```

/* In the opening and middlegame, the king is stronger in or adjacent to a corner on its side of the board. It tends to be weaker on a more central file. Beyond the 2nd rank, it tends to be very weak. The -48 score is somewhat arbitrary. */

```
int king_endgame_score[64] =
{
```

```
    0,    8,   16,   18,   18,   16,   8,    0,
    8,   16,   24,   32,   32,   24,  16,    8,
   16,   24,   32,   40,   40,   32,  24,   16,
   25,   32,   40,   48,   48,   40,  32,   25,
   25,   32,   40,   48,   48,   40,  32,   25,
   16,   24,   32,   40,   40,   32,  24,   16,
    8,   16,   24,   32,   32,   24,  16,    8,
    0,    8,   16,   18,   18,   16,   8,    0
};
```

/* In the endgame, the king is stronger as it gets closer to the centre. */

```
int passed_score[64] =
{
    0,    0, 0,    0,   0,   0, 0,  0,
    0,    0, 0,    0,   0,   0, 0,  0,
   60,   60, 60,  60,  60,  60, 60, 60,
   30,   30, 30,  30,  30,  30, 30, 30,
   15,   15, 15,  15,  15,  15, 15, 15,
    8,    8,  8,   8,   8,   8,  8,  8,
    8,    8,  8,   8,   8,   8,  8,  8,
    0,    0,  0,   0,   0,   0,  0,  0
};
```

/* The value of a passed pawn depends on the rank it is on. The more advanced they are, the more they are worth. The more advanced they are, the bigger the difference between ranks. For example, the difference between the 4th and 5th ranks is 15, while the difference between the 5th and 6th ranks is 30.

The 2nd and 3rd ranks are worth the same because of the double pawn move. Note that the 7th rank is omitted because pawns there are always passed and are handled by the pawn_score table. */

```
int castle_mask[64] =
{
   13, 15, 15, 15, 12, 15, 15, 14,
   15, 15, 15, 15, 15, 15, 15, 15,
   15, 15, 15, 15, 15, 15, 15, 15,
   15, 15, 15, 15, 15, 15, 15, 15,
   15, 15, 15, 15, 15, 15, 15, 15,
   15, 15, 15, 15, 15, 15, 15, 15,
   15, 15, 15, 15, 15, 15, 15, 15,
```

```
   7,  15,  15,  15,   3,  15,  15,  11
};
```

/* Note that most squares in **castle_mask** have a value of 15, and the matching bit in **castle** remains that way. The only bits that are changed are the starting squares of the kings and rooks. If the king moves, then castling becomes impossible for that player. If a rook moves or is captured, then castling on that side becomes impossible for that player. This code comes from TSCP by Tom Kerrigan. */

```
int rank[2][64];
```

/* The rank array returns the rank from the player's side. For white, it is unchanged. For black, it is 7 minus the rank.

SetTables()

SetTables() fills the **square_score** tables with the individual piece tables. The value of each piece is added to the score for each square. The board is flipped for the Black scores. */

```
void SetTables()
{
  for (int x = 0; x < 64; x++)
  {
    square_score[White][P][x] = pawn_score[x] +
piece_value[P];
    square_score[White][N][x] = knight_score[x] +
piece_value[N];
    square_score[White][B][x] = bishop_score[x] +
piece_value[B];
    square_score[White][R][x] = rook_score[x] +
piece_value[R];
    square_score[White][Q][x] = queen_score[x] +
piece_value[Q];
    square_score[White][K][x] = king_score[x];
    square_score[Black][P][x] = pawn_score[Flip[x]] +
piece_value[P];
    square_score[Black][N][x] = knight_score[Flip[x]]
+ piece_value[N];
    square_score[Black][B][x] = bishop_score[Flip[x]]
+ piece_value[B];
```

```
    square_score[Black][R][x] = rook_score[Flip[x]] +
piece_value[R];
    square_score[Black][Q][x] = queen_score[Flip[x]] +
piece_value[Q];
    square_score[Black][K][x] = king_score[Flip[x]];
    king_endgame[White][x] = king_endgame_score[x] -
square_score[White][K][x];
    king_endgame[Black][x] = king_endgame_score[x] -
square_score[Black][K][x];
    passed[White][x] = passed_score[Flip[x]];
    passed[Black][x] = passed_score[x];
  }
}
```

InitBoard()

/* **InitBoard()** sets up variables for a new game. */

```
void InitBoard()
{
  memset(bit_pieces, 0, sizeof(bit_pieces));
  memset(bit_units, 0, sizeof(bit_units));
  bit_all = 0;
  for (int x = 0; x < 64; x++)
  {
    board[x] = EMPTY;
  }
  for (int x = 0; x < 64; ++x)
  {
    if (init_board[x] != EMPTY)
      AddPiece(init_color[x], init_board[x], x);
  }
  side = White;
  xside = Black;
  fifty = 0;
  castle = 15;
  ply = 0;
  hply = 0;
  first_move[0] = 0;
  turn = 0;
}
```

NewPosition()

/* **NewPosition()** gets the board ready before the computer starts to think. */

```
void NewPosition()
{
  memset(pawn_mat, 0, sizeof(pawn_mat));
  memset(piece_mat, 0, sizeof(piece_mat));
  for (int i = 0; i < 64; i++)
  {
    if (board[i] != EMPTY)
    {
      if (bit_units[White] & mask[i])
        AddPiece(White, board[i], i);
      if (bit_units[Black] & mask[i])
        AddPiece(Black, board[i], i);
    }
  }
  currentkey = GetKey();
  currentlock = GetLock();
}
```

Algebraic()

/* **Algebraic()** displays a square.
e.g. 3 becomes col[3] + 96 which is ASCII character **d** and
row[3]+1 which is **1**. Passing 3 returns **d1**. */

```
void Algebraic(int a)
{
  if (a < 0 || a > 63) return;
  char c[2] = "a";
  c[0] = 96 + 1 + col[a];
  printf("%s%d", c, row[a] + 1);
}
```

Alg()

/* **Alg()** displays a move. */

```
void Alg(int a,int b)
{
  Algebraic(a);
  Algebraic(b);
}
```

SetMoves()

/* **SetMoves()** creates the lookup tables for piece moves. */

```
void SetMoves()
{
  SetKnightMoves();
  SetLinePieces();
  SetKingMoves();
}
```

SetKnightMoves()

/* **SetKnightMoves()** prefills the lookup tables for knights. These will later be used to generate moves, captures and attacks. **if** statements are used to stop knights from moving off the board. */

```
static void SetKnightMoves()
{
  for (int x = 0; x < 64; x++)
  {
    bit_moves[N][x] = 0;
    if (row[x] < 6 && col[x] < 7)
      bit_moves[N][x] |= mask[x + 17];
    if (row[x] < 7 && col[x] < 6)
      bit_moves[N][x] |= mask[x + 10];
    if (row[x] < 6 && col[x] > 0)
      bit_moves[N][x] |= mask[x + 15];
    if (row[x] < 7 && col[x] > 1)
      bit_moves[N][x] |= mask[x + 6];
    if (row[x] > 1 && col[x] < 7)
      bit_moves[N][x] |= mask[x - 15];
    if (row[x] > 0 && col[x] < 6)
      bit_moves[N][x] |= mask[x - 6];
    if (row[x] > 1 && col[x] > 0)
      bit_moves[N][x] |= mask[x - 17];
    if (row[x] > 0 && col[x] > 1)
      bit_moves[N][x] |= mask[x - 10];
  }
}
```

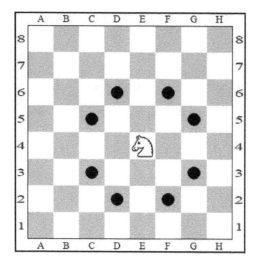

/*

```
0 0 0 0 0 0 0 0
0 0 0 0 0 0 0 0
0 0 0 1 0 1 0 0
0 0 1 0 0 0 1 0
0 0 0 0 0 0 0 0
0 0 1 0 0 0 1 0
0 0 0 1 0 1 0 0
0 0 0 0 0 0 0 0
```

This bitboard stores the knight moves from **e4**.

SetLinePieces()

All 64 squares of the board are traversed and compared with every other square.

- If squares are on the same diagonal, they are added to bishop moves.
- If squares are on the same rank or file, they are added to rook moves.
- If squares are on the same rank, file or diagonal, they are added to queen moves.

```
*/

static void SetLinePieces()
{
  for (int x = 0; x < 64; x++)
  {
    bit_moves[B][x] = 0;
    bit_moves[R][x] = 0;
    bit_moves[Q][x] = 0;
    for (int y = 0; y < 64; y++)
    {
      if (x == y)
        continue;
      if (nwdiag[x] == nwdiag[y] || nediag[x] ==
nediag[y])
        bit_moves[B][x] |= mask[y];
      if (row[x] == row[y] || col[x] == col[y])
        bit_moves[R][x] |= mask[y];
      if (nwdiag[x] == nwdiag[y] || nediag[x] ==
nediag[y] ||
row[x] == row[y] || col[x] == col[y])
        bit_moves[Q][x] |= mask[y];
    }
  }
}

/*
```

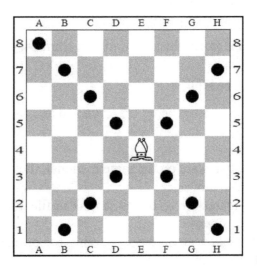

```
1 0 0 0 0 0 0 0
0 1 0 0 0 0 0 1
0 0 1 0 0 0 1 0
0 0 0 1 0 1 0 0
0 0 0 0 0 0 0 0
0 0 0 1 0 1 0 0
0 0 1 0 0 0 1 0
0 1 0 0 0 0 0 1
```

This bitboard stores the bishop moves from e4.

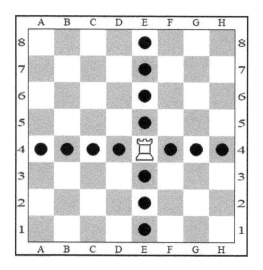

```
0 0 0 0 1 0 0 0
0 0 0 0 1 0 0 0
0 0 0 0 1 0 0 0
0 0 0 0 1 0 0 0
1 1 1 1 0 1 1 1
0 0 0 0 1 0 0 0
0 0 0 0 1 0 0 0
0 0 0 0 1 0 0 0
```

This bitboard stores the rook moves from e4.

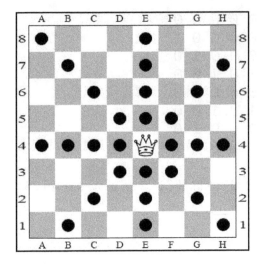

```
1 0 0 0 1 0 0 0
0 1 0 0 1 0 0 1
0 0 1 0 1 0 1 0
0 0 0 1 1 1 0 0
1 1 1 1 0 1 1 1
0 0 0 1 1 1 1 0
0 0 1 0 1 0 1 0
0 1 0 0 1 0 0 1
```

This bitboard stores the queen moves from e4.

SetKingMoves()

SetKingMoves() prefills the lookup tables for kings. These will later be used to generate moves, captures and attacks. **if** statements are used to stop kings from moving off the board. */

```
static void SetKingMoves()
{
  for (int x = 0; x < 64; x++)
  {
    if (col[x] > 0)
      bit_moves[K][x] |= mask[x - 1];
    if (col[x] < 7)
      bit_moves[K][x] |= mask[x + 1];
    if (row[x] > 0)
      bit_moves[K][x] |= mask[x - 8];
```

```
    if (row[x] < 7)
      bit_moves[K][x] |= mask[x + 8];
    if (col[x] < 7 && row[x] < 7)
      bit_moves[K][x] |= mask[x + 9];
    if (col[x] > 0 && row[x] < 7)
      bit_moves[K][x] |= mask[x + 7];
    if (col[x] > 0 && row[x] > 0)
      bit_moves[K][x] |= mask[x - 9];
    if (col[x] < 7 && row[x]>0)
      bit_moves[K][x] |= mask[x - 7];
  }
}
```

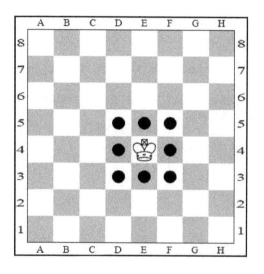

/*

```
0 0 0 0 0 0 0 0
0 0 0 0 0 0 0 0
0 0 0 0 0 0 0 0
0 0 0 1 1 1 0 0
0 0 0 1 0 1 0 0
0 0 0 1 1 1 0 0
0 0 0 0 0 0 0 0
0 0 0 0 0 0 0 0
```

This bitboard stores the king moves from e4. */

attack.cpp

```
#include "globals.h"
```

Attack()

/* **Attack()** returns *true* if one side attacks a given square and *false* if it doesn't. It is used to tell if a king is in check, but it can have other uses. */

```
bool Attack(const int s, const int sq)
{
  if (bit_pawndefends[s][sq] & bit_pieces[s][P])
    return true;
  if (bit_moves[N][sq] & bit_pieces[s][N])
    return true;
  BITBOARD b1 = bit_moves[R][sq] & (bit_pieces[s][R] |
bit_pieces[s][Q]);
  b1 |= (bit_moves[B][sq] & (bit_pieces[s][B] |
bit_pieces[s][Q]));
  while (b1)
  {
    int sq2 = NextBit(b1);
    if (!(bit_between[sq2][sq] & bit_all))
      return true;
    b1 &= b1 - 1;
  }
  if (bit_moves[K][sq] & bit_pieces[s][K])
    return true;
  return false;
}
```

/* Attackers are searched for in order of strength, starting with pawns and knights. Both attacking pawns and knights are searched for with a single **if** statement.

A bitboard **b1** is created representing the bishops, rooks and queens that might be attacking. Rooks and Queens are searched for on ranks and files extending from the square. Bishops and Queens are also searched for on diagonals extending from the square.

If there are no units between the potential attacker and the attacked square then **Attack()** returns true.

LowestAttacker

LowestAttacker() is similar to **Attack**. It returns the square that the weakest attacker is on. It returns -1 if there are no attackers. It is used to find the next piece that may recapture, in a recapturing sequence. It may have other uses. */

```
int LowestAttacker(const int s, const int xs, const
int sq)
{
  if (bit_left[xs][sq] & bit_pieces[s][P])
    return pawnleft[xs][sq];
  if (bit_right[xs][sq] & bit_pieces[s][P])
    return pawnright[xs][sq];
  BITBOARD b1;
  b1 = bit_moves[N][sq] & bit_pieces[s][N];
  if (b1)
    return NextBit(b1);
  for (int piece = B; piece < K; piece++)
  {
    b1 = bit_moves[piece][sq] & bit_pieces[s][piece];
    while (b1)
    {
      int sq2 = NextBit(b1);
      if (!(bit_between[sq2][sq] & bit_all))
        return sq2;
      b1 &= b1 - 1;
    }
  }
  b1 = bit_moves[K][sq] & bit_pieces[s][K];
  if (b1)
    return NextBit(b1);
  return -1;
}
```

/* Note that **bit_between** is used to see if a bishop, rook or queen is blocked. */

gen.cpp

```
#include "globals.h"
move *g;
```

/* This is a pointer to a move structure that stores generated moves. */

```
static int matrix[6][6] = {
{0,10,20,30,40,0}//pawn captures
,{-3,7,17,27,37,0}//knight captures
,{-3,7,17,27,37,0}//bishop captures
,{-5,5,15,25,35,0}//rook captures
,{-9,1,11,21,31,0}//queen captures
,{0,10,20,30,40,0}//pawn captures
};
```

/* These tables contain scores for captures by and of different pieces. They are used to help sort captures. The capturing piece is represented by the name of the array. The captured piece represents the index. MV-LA (most valuable capture, least valuable attacker) is used.

For example, A rook capturing a bishop is **matrix[3][2]**, which is 15.

The captures are in order.

- P x Q, N or B x Q, R X Q
- P x R, N or B x R, R X R
- P x N, N or B x N, R X N
- P x P, N or B x P, R X P

Captures by the king get a high score because the captured piece is undefended (otherwise it's illegal). */

```
int ForwardSquare[2] = {8,-8};
```

/* **ForwardSquare** is the change in the square number when a pawn moves forward. The square number for White is increased by 8, while the square number for Black is decreased by 8.

Gen()

move_count = first_move[ply] sets the first move of the move list to the end of the previous list.

It then sees if an *en passant* capture or castling is possible.

It then loops through the different types of pieces of the side to move and generates moves for them. For bishops, rooks and queens, it generates moves in each possible direction. */

```
void Gen(const int s, const int xs)
{
  int i, j, n;
  BITBOARD b1, b2, b3;
  move_count = first_move[ply];
  GenEp(s);
  GenCastle(s);
  if (s == White)
  {
    b1 = bit_pieces[White][P] & ((bit_units[Black] &
not_h_file) >> 7);
    b2 = bit_pieces[White][P] & ((bit_units[Black] &
not_a_file) >> 9);
    b3 = bit_pieces[White][P] & ~(bit_all >> 8);
  }
  else
  {
    b1 = bit_pieces[Black][P] & ((bit_units[White] &
not_h_file) << 9);
    b2 = bit_pieces[Black][P] & ((bit_units[White] &
not_a_file) << 7);
    b3 = bit_pieces[Black][P] & ~(bit_all << 8);
  }
```

/* **b1 = bit_pieces[White][P] & ((bit_units[1] & not_h_file) >> 7)**
This creates a bitboard of captures to the left.

b2 = bit_pieces[White][P] & ((bit_units[Black] & not_a_file) >> 9)
This creates a bitboard of captures to the right.

b3 = bit_pieces[White][P] & ~(bit_all >> 8) This creates a bitboard of unblocked pawns.

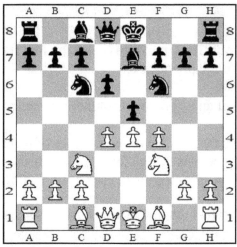

White to move has left and right pawn captures.

```
0 0 0 0 0 0 0 0
0 0 0 0 0 0 0 0
0 0 0 0 0 0 0 0
0 0 0 0 0 0 0 0
0 0 0 0 0 1 0 0
0 0 0 0 0 0 0 0
0 0 0 0 0 0 0 0
0 0 0 0 0 0 0 0
```

This is the bitboard of pawns that can capture to the left.

```
0 0 0 0 0 0 0 0
0 0 0 0 0 0 0 0
0 0 0 0 0 0 0 0
0 0 0 0 0 0 0 0
0 0 0 1 0 0 0 0
0 0 0 0 0 0 0 0
0 0 0 0 0 0 0 0
0 0 0 0 0 0 0 0
```

This is the bitboard of pawns that can capture to the right.

```
0 0 0 0 0 0 0 0
0 0 0 0 0 0 0 0
0 0 0 0 0 0 0 0
0 0 0 0 0 0 0 0
0 0 0 1 0 1 0 0
0 0 0 0 0 0 0 0
1 1 0 0 0 0 1 1
0 0 0 0 0 0 0 0
```

This is the bitboard of pawns that can move forward. */

```
while (b1)
{
  sq = NextBit(b1);
  b1 &= b1 - 1;
  sq2 = pawnleft[s][sq];
  if (rank[side][sq] == 6)
    AddPromoteCapture(sq, sq2, matrix[P][board[sq2]]);
  else
    AddCapture(sq, sq2, matrix[P][board[sq2]]);
}
while (b2)
{
  sq = NextBit(b2);
  b2 &= b2 - 1;
  sq2 = pawnright[s][sq];
  if (rank[side][sq] == 6)
    AddPromoteCapture(sq, sq2, matrix[P][board[sq2]]);
  else
    AddCapture(sq, sq2, matrix[P][board[sq2]]);
}
```

/* The left and right pawn captures are added to the move list with **AddCapture**. */

```
  while (b3)
  {
    sq = NextBit(b3);
    b3 &= b3 - 1;
    if(rank[side][sq] == 6)
      AddMove(sq, pawnplus[side][sq], PROMOTE);
    else
      AddMove(sq, pawnplus[side][sq],0);
    if (rank[s][sq] == 1 && board[pawndouble[s][sq]]
```

```
== EMPTY)
    {
      AddMove(sq, pawndouble[s][sq],0);
    }
  }
```

/* The single and double pawn moves are added to the move list with **AddMove**. */

```
b1 = bit_pieces[s][N];
while (b1)
{
  sq = NextBit(b1);
  b1 &= b1 - 1;
  b2 = bit_moves[N][sq] & bit_units[xs];
  while (b2)
  {
    sq2 = NextBit(b2);
    b2 &= b2 - 1;
    AddCapture(sq, sq2, matrix[sq2][board[sq2]]);
  }
  b2 = bit_moves[N][sq] & ~bit_all;
  while (b2)
  {
    sq2 = NextBit(b2);
    b2 &= b2 - 1;
    AddMove(sq, sq2, 0);
  }
}

/*
```

```
0 0 0 0 0 0 0 0
0 0 0 0 0 0 0 0
0 0 0 0 0 0 0 0
0 1 0 1 0 0 0 0
1 0 0 0 0 0 0 0
0 0 0 0 0 0 0 0
0 0 0 0 1 0 0 0
0 1 0 0 0 0 0 0
```

This is the bitboard of non-capturing moves of the white queen knight. **b1** is a bitboard representing the knights of the side to move. The knights are looped through. All captures are generated by combining knight moves from the square with opponent units. All other moves are generated by combining knight moves from the square with empty squares.

The line pieces are done similarly. **b1** is a bitboard representing the pieces of the moving side.

The piece types are looped through.

Pieces of the same type are looped through with the **while(b1)** loop.

A bitboard **b2** is created, storing the possible squares a piece could move to.

Squares blocked by friendly units and squares after them are removed with the **while(b3)** loop.

Captures are generated and squares after them are removed with the second **while(b3)** loop.

The **while(b2)** loop adds the moves left over. */

```
int sq2;
for(int piece=B;piece<=Q;piece++)
{
b1 = bit_pieces[s][piece];
while(b1)
{
  sq = NextBit(b1);
  b1 &= b1 - 1;
  b2 = bit_moves[piece][sq];
  b3 = b2 & bit_units[s];
  while(b3)
  {
    sq2 = NextBit(b3);
    b3 &= bit_after[sq][sq2];
    b2 &= bit_after[sq][sq2];
  }
  b3 = b2 & bit_units[xs];
  while(b3)
```

```
    {
      sq2 = NextBit(b3);
      if(!(bit_between[sq][sq2] & bit_all))
      {
        AddCapture(sq,sq2,matrix[piece][board[sq2]]);
      }
      b3 &= bit_after[sq][sq2];
      b2 &= bit_after[sq][sq2];
    }
    while(b2)
    {
      sq2 = NextBit(b2);
      b2 &= not_mask[sq2];
      AddMove(sq,sq2);
    }
  }
}
```

/* This generates moves for bishops, rooks and queens. */

```
i = NextBit(bit_pieces[s][K]);
b1 = bit_moves[K][i] & bit_units[xs];
while(b1)
{
  n = NextBit(b1);
  b1 &= b1 - 1;
  AddCapture(i,n,matrix[K][board[n]]);
}
b1 = bit_moves[K][i] & ~bit_all;
while(b1)
{
  n = NextBit(b1);
  b1 &= b1 - 1;
  AddMove(i,n);
}
first_move[ply + 1] = move_count;
}
```

/* This generates moves for the king.

```
0 0 0 0 0 0 0 0
0 0 0 0 0 0 0 0
0 0 0 0 0 0 0 0
0 0 0 0 0 0 0 0
0 0 0 0 0 0 0 0
```

```
0 0 0 0 0 0 0 0
0 0 0 1 1 1 0 0
0 0 0 0 0 0 0 0
```

This is the bitboard of the moves of the white king.

GenEp()

GenEp() looks at the last move played and sees if it is a double pawn move. If so, it sees if there is an opponent pawn next to it. If there is, it adds the *en passant* capture to the move list. */

```
static void GenEp(const int s)
{
  int ep = game_list[hply - 1].to;
  if (board[ep] == P && abs(game_list[hply - 1].from -
ep) == 16)
  {
    if (col[ep] > 0 && mask[ep - 1] & bit_pieces[s]
[P])
      AddEP(ep - 1, pawnplus[side][ep]);
    if (col[ep] < 7 && mask[ep + 1] & bit_pieces[s]
[P])
      AddEP(ep + 1, pawnplus[side][ep]);
  }
}
```

/* Note that sometimes two *en passant* captures are possible.

GenCastle()

GenCastle() generates a castling move if the king and rook have not moved and there are no pieces in the way. Attacked squares between the king and the rook are dealt with in **MakeMove()**. */

```
static void GenCastle(const int s)
{
  if (s == White)
  {
    if (castle & CASTLE_G1 && !(bit_between[H1][E1] &
bit_all))
      AddMove(E1, G1, CASTLE);
    if (castle & CASTLE_C1 && !(bit_between[A1][E1] &
```

```
bit_all))
      AddMove(E1, C1, CASTLE);
  }
  else
  {
    if (castle & CASTLE_G8 && !(bit_between[E8][H8] &
bit_all))
      AddMove(E8, G8, CASTLE);
    if (castle & CASTLE_C8 && !(bit_between[E8][A8] &
bit_all))
      AddMove(E8, C8, CASTLE);
  }
}

/*
```

castle & CASTLE_G1 tests to see whether white can castle kingside.
castle & CASTLE_C1 tests to see whether white can castle queenside.
castle & CASTLE_G8 tests to see whether black can castle kingside.
castle & CASTLE_C8 tests to see whether black can castle queenside.

AddMove() adds the from and to squares of a move to the move list.
The score is the **history** value.
The move count, **move_count**, is incremented.

AddMove()

```
*/

static void AddMove(const int x, const int sq, const
int flags)
{
  move_list[move_count].from = x;
  move_list[move_count].to = sq;
  move_list[move_count].score = history[x][sq];
  move_list[move_count].flags = flags;
  move_count++;
}
```

AddCapture()

/* **AddCapture()** adds the from and to squares of a move to the movelist.
CAPTURE_SCORE is added to the score so that captures will be looked at first.
The score is also added and will be used in move ordering.
The move count, **move_count** is incremented as with **AddMove()**.
*/

```
static void AddCapture(const int x, const int sq,
const int score)
{
  move_list[move_count].from = x;
  move_list[move_count].to = sq;
  move_list[move_count].flags = CAPTURE;
  move_list[move_count].score = score + CAPTURE_SCORE;
  move_count++;
}
```

AddPromoteCapture()

/* **AddPromoteCapture()** adds pawn promotions that are also captures. */

```
static void AddPromoteCapture(const int x, const int
sq, const int score)
{
  move_list[move_count].from = x;
  move_list[move_count].to = sq;
  move_list[move_count].flags = CAPTURE | PROMOTE;
  move_list[move_count].score = score + CAPTURE_SCORE;
  move_count++;
}
```

AddEP()

/* **AddEP()** adds *en passant* captures. */

```
static void AddEP(const int x, const int sq)
{
  move_list[move_count].from = x;
  move_list[move_count].to = sq;
  move_list[move_count].flags = EP;
```

```
  move_list[move_count].score = 10 + CAPTURE_SCORE;
  move_count++;
}
```

GenCaptures()

/* **GenCaptures()** is similar to Gen, except that only captures are
being generated instead of all moves. Captures by pawns, knights
and kings are done in the same way as when all moves are
generated. */

```
void GenCaptures(const int s, const int xs)
{
  move_count = first_move[ply];
  int sq, sq2, n;
  BITBOARD b1, b2;
  if (s == White)
  {
    b1 = bit_pieces[White][P] & ((bit_units[Black] &
not_h_file) >> 7);
    b2 = bit_pieces[White][P] & ((bit_units[Black] &
not_a_file) >> 9);
  }
  else
  {
    b1 = bit_pieces[Black][P] & ((bit_units[White] &
not_h_file << 9);
    b2 = bit_pieces[Black][P] & ((bit_units[White] &
not_a_file) << 7);
  }
  while (b1)
  {
    sq = NextBit(b1);
    b1 &= b1 - 1;
    n = pawnleft[s][sq];
    AddCapture(sq, n, matrix[P][board[n]]);
  }
  while (b2)
  {
    sq = NextBit(b2);
    b2 &= b2 - 1;
    n = pawnright[s][sq];
    AddCapture(sq, n, matrix[P][board[n]]);
  }
```

/* Pawn captures are generated in the same way they are in **Gen()**.
*/

```
b1 = bit_pieces[s][N];
while (b1)
{
  sq = NextBit(b1);
  b1 &= b1 - 1;
  b2 = bit_moves[N][sq] & bit_units[xs];
  while (b2)
  {
    sq2 = NextBit(b2);
    b2 &= b2 - 1;
    AddCapture(sq, sq2, matrix[1][board[sq2]]);
  }
}
```

/* Knight captures are generated and added to the move list with
AddCapture(). */

```
for (int piece = B; piece <= Q; piece++)
{
  b1 = bit_pieces[s][piece];
  while (b1)
  {
    sq = NextBit(b1);
    b1 &= b1 - 1;
    b2 = bit_moves[piece][sq] & bit_units[xs];
    while (b2)
    {
      sq2 = NextBit(b2);
      if (!(bit_between[sq][sq2] & bit_all))
        AddCapture(sq, sq2, matrix[piece]
[board[sq2]]);
      b2 &= bit_after[sq2];
    }
  }
}
```

/* Captures for the line pieces are done differently. Bishop, rook
and queen captures are generated and added to the move list with
AddCapture(). The statement **b2 = bit_moves[piece][sq] &
bit_units[xs];** creates a bitboard of all the opponent pieces
attacked by the piece. This bitboard is looped through one square

at a time.

Note that for bishops, rooks and queens that **bit_between** is used to test whether the line is blocked or not. **b2 &= bit_after[sq2];** clears both the bit representing the square the captured piece is on and the squares behind it.

The statement **if(!(bit_between[sq][sq2] & bit_all)) AddCapture(sq,sq2,bx[board[sq2]]);** adds a capture, only if there are no units of either side between **sq** (the attacking square) and **sq2** (the attacked square).

This is the position from the famous Lasker-Bauer game in which, instead of playing the obvious capture of the Knight, Lasker played a double bishop sacrifice starting with **1.Bxh7+**.

```
0 0 0 0 0 0 0 0
0 0 0 0 1 0 0 0
1 0 0 0 1 0 0 0
0 0 0 0 0 0 0 1
0 0 0 0 0 0 0 0
0 0 0 0 0 0 0 0
0 0 0 0 0 0 0 0
0 0 0 0 0 0 0 0
```

This is the bitboard of possible white queen captures.

The **bit_between[sq][sq2] & bit_all** test fails for a6, e6 and e7, so the only legal capture is e2h5.

Queen captures are generated and added to the move list with **AddCapture()**. Notes that when e6 is cleared, **bit_after** also clears e7. */

```
sq = NextBit(bit_pieces[s][K]);
b2 = bit_moves[K][sq] & bit_units[xs];
while(b2)
{
  sq2 = NextBit(b2);
  b2 &= b2 - 1;
  AddCapture(sq,sq2,matrix[K][board[sq2]]);
}
first_move[ply + 1] = move_count;
}

/*
```

King captures are generated and added to the move list with **AddCapture()**.

first_move[ply] is the starting point of the move list for the current ply. **first_move[ply+1]** is the starting point of the move list for the next ply. **first_move[ply+1]** is assigned the value of **move_count** (the move count).

For example, in the initial position, there are 20 legal moves and 20 legal replies.
first_move[0] has a value of zero.
first_move[1] has a value of 20.
first_move[2] has a value of 40. */

update.cpp

```
#include "globals.h"
game_data* g;
```

/* This is a pointer to a move structure that stores game list moves.

UpdatePiece()

UpdatePiece() updates the Hash Table key with **AddKey()** and the board, whenever a piece moves.
board is updated.
The square the piece moved from is removed from **bit_pieces**.
The square moved to is added to **bit_pieces**. */

```
static void UpdatePiece(const int s, const int piece,
const int from, const int to)
{
  AddKey(s, piece, from);
  AddKey(s, piece, to);
  board[to] = piece;
  board[from] = EMPTY;
  bit_pieces[s][piece] &= not_mask[from];
  bit_pieces[s][piece] |= mask[to];
  bit_units[s] &= not_mask[from];
  bit_units[s] |= mask[to];
  bit_all = bit_units[White] | bit_units[Black];
}
```

/* **bit_units** and **bit_all** are modified.

RemovePiece

RemovePiece() updates the Hash Table key and the board whenever a piece is removed.
The square the piece is on is removed from **bit_pieces**.
bit_units and **bit_all** are also modified. */

```
void RemovePiece(const int s, const int piece, const
int sq)
```

```
{
  AddKey(s, piece, sq);
  board[sq] = EMPTY;
  bit_pieces[s][piece] &= not_mask[sq];
  bit_units[s] &= not_mask[sq];
  bit_all = bit_units[White] | bit_units[Black];
}
```

AddPiece

/* **AddPiece()** updates the Hash Table key and the board whenever a piece is added.
The square the piece is on is added to **bit_pieces**.
bit_units and **bit_all** are also modified. */

```
void AddPiece(const int s, const int piece, const int sq)
{
  board[sq] = piece;
  AddKey(s, piece, sq);
  bit_pieces[s][piece] |= mask[sq];
  bit_units[s] |= mask[sq];
  bit_all = bit_units[0] | bit_units[1];
}
```

MakeMove

/* **MakeMove()** updates the board whenever a move is made. */

```
int MakeMove(move_data m)
{
  const int from = m.from;
  const int to = m.to;
  const int flags = m.flags;
  if (flags & CASTLE)
  {
    if (Attack(xside, from))
      return false;
    if (to == G1)
    {
      if (Attack(xside, F1))
        return false;
      UpdatePiece(side, R, H1, F1);
    }
```

```
      else if (to == C1)
      {
        if (Attack(xside, D1))
          return false;
        UpdatePiece(side, R, A1, D1);
      }
      else if (to == G8)
      {
        if (Attack(xside, F8))
          return false;
        UpdatePiece(side, R, H8, F8);
      }
      else if (to == C8)
      {
        if (Attack(xside, D8))
          return false;
        UpdatePiece(side, R, A8, D8);
      }
    }
    g = &game_list[hply];
    g->from = from;
    g->to = to;
    g->flags = flags;
    g->capture = board[to];
    g->castle = castle;
    g->fifty = fifty;
    g->hash = currentkey;
    g->lock = currentlock;
    g->castle = castle;
    castle &= castle_mask[from] & castle_mask[to];
    ply++;
    hply++;
    fifty++;
    if (board[from] == P)
    {
      fifty = 0;
      if (flags & EP)
      {
        RemovePiece(xside, P, pawnplus[xside][to]);
      }
    }
    if (flags & CAPTURE)
    {
      fifty = 0;
      RemovePiece(xside, board[to], to);
    }
    if (flags & PROMOTE)
```

```
    {
      RemovePiece(side, P, from);
      AddPiece(side, Q, to);
    }
    else
    {
      UpdatePiece(side, board[from], from, to);
    }
    side ^= 1;
    xside ^= 1;
    if (Attack(side, NextBit(bit_pieces[xside][K])))
    {
      UnMakeMove();
      return false;
    }
    return true;
}
```

/* If a pawn moves, then the fifty-move count is reset to zero. If a pawn moves and changes files without making a capture, then it's an *en passant* capture, and the captured pawn is removed. */

```
if(board[to] != EMPTY)
{
  fifty = 0;
  RemovePiece(xside,board[to],to);
}
```

/* If the move is a capture, then the captured piece is removed from the board, and the fifty-move count is reset to zero. */

```
if(board[from]==P && (row[to]==0 || row[to]==7))
{
  RemovePiece(side, P, from);
  AddPiece(side, Q, to);
  g- > promote = Q;
}
else
{
  g- > promote = 0;
  UpdatePiece(side,board[from],from,to);
}
```

/* If a pawn moves to the last rank, then it's promoted. The pawn is removed, and a queen is added. For simplicity, the engine does not look at under promotions. 999 times out of 1000 is best to promote to a queen. However, the engine will recognise when the opponent has under-promoted. */

```
side ^= 1;
xside ^= 1;
```

/* Sides are switched. **side** and **xside** are either 0 or 1. ^= tuens 0 into 1, and 1 into 0. */

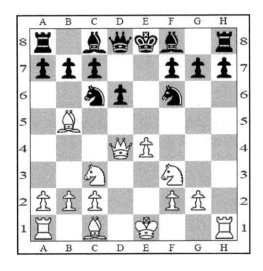

```
if(Attack(side,NextBit(bit_pieces[xside][K])))
{
   TakeBack();
   return false;
}
```

/* If the move leaves the king in check (for example, if a pinned piece moved), then the move is taken back. Black plays **1...Nxd4**. However, the Knight is pinned to the King, so Nxd4 leaves the Black King in check. Black has to take back **1...Nxd4**. */

```
return true;
}
```

UnMakeMove

/* **UnMakeMove()** is the opposite of **MakeMove()**, though in some ways simpler.

- Sides are flipped.
- If the move was an *en passant* capture, the captured pawn is replaced.
- If the move was a promotion, the promotion piece is replaced and a pawn added.
- Otherwise, the moving piece is updated.
- If the move was a capture, the captured piece is replaced.
- If castling is unmade, the rook is returned to its own square.

*/

```
void UnMakeMove()
{
  side ^= 1;
  xside ^= 1;
  ply--;
  hply--;
  game_data* m = &game_list[hply];
  int from = m->from;
  int to = m->to;
  int flags = m->flags;
  castle = m->castle;
  if (flags & EP)
    AddPiece(xside, P, pawnplus[xside][to]);
  if (flags & PROMOTE)
  {
    AddPiece(side, P, from);
    RemovePiece(side, board[to], to);
  }
  else
    UpdatePiece(side, board[to], to, from);
  if (flags & CAPTURE)
    AddPiece(xside, m->capture, to);
  if (flags & CASTLE)
  {
    if (to == G1)
      UpdatePiece(side, R, F1, H1);
    else if (to == C1)
      UpdatePiece(side, R, D1, A1);
```

```
      else if (to == G8)
        UpdatePiece(side, R, F8, H8);
      else if (to == C8)
        UpdatePiece(side, R, D8, A8);
  }
}
```

MakeRecapture

/* **MakeRecapture()** is simpler than **MakeMove()** because there is no castling involved, and it doesn't include *en passant* capture and promotion.

If the capture is illegal, it is taken back. This may happen because the capturing piece was pinned to the king or a previous capture created a discovered check. */

```
int MakeRecapture(const int from, const int to)
{
  game_list[hply].from = from;
  game_list[hply].to = to;
  game_list[hply].capture = board[to];
  ++ply;
  ++hply;
  RemovePiece(xside, board[to], to);
  UpdatePiece(side, board[from], from, to);
  side ^= 1;
  xside ^= 1;
  if (Attack(side, NextBit(bit_pieces[xside][K])))
  {
    UnMakeRecapture();
    return false;
  }
  return true;
}
```

UnMakeRecapture

/* **UnMakeRecapture()** is very similar to MakeRecapture. Sides are flipped, and ply and hply are decremented. The capturing piece returns to where it came from, and the captured piece is added to the board. */

```
void UnMakeRecapture()
{
  side ^= 1;
  xside ^= 1;
  --ply;
  --hply;
  UpdatePiece(side, board[game_list[hply].to],
game_list[hply].to, game_list[hply].from);
  AddPiece(xside, game_list[hply].capture,
game_list[hply].to);
}
```

Eval.cpp

Evaluation

The evaluation function creates scores of the position for both sides. It is from the point of view of the side that has just moved. The final score is this side's score minus the other side's score.

The maximum possible score is 10,000, which represents giving checkmate. The minimum possible score is -10,000, which represents being checkmated. Other scores are between these extremes. Zero represents an equal position.

The basic unit is a pawn, which is worth 100 points or centipawns. The total material of one side is worth 3200 points. The king has no score because it is never captured.

```
#include "globals.h"
```

/* An isolated pawn has a negative value of 20. */

```
#define ISOLATED 20
int queenside_pawns[2],kingside_pawns[2];
extern BITBOARD mask_kingside;
extern BITBOARD mask_queenside;
```

/* In the middlegame, pawns may help protect the King. **queenside_defence** stores values for pawn position if a king is on the queenside. There is a score for pawns being on the 2nd or 3rd rank. */

```
const int queenside_defence[2][64]=
{
{
  0, 0, 0, 0, 0, 0, 0, 0,
  8,10, 8, 0, 0, 0, 0, 0,
  8, 6, 8, 0, 0, 0, 0, 0,
  0, 0, 0, 0, 0, 0, 0, 0,
  0, 0, 0, 0, 0, 0, 0, 0,
```

```
  0,  0,  0,  0,  0,  0,  0,  0,
  0,  0,  0,  0,  0,  0,  0,  0,
  0,  0,  0,  0,  0,  0,  0,  0
},
{
  0,  0,  0,  0,  0,  0,  0,  0,
  0,  0,  0,  0,  0,  0,  0,  0,
  0,  0,  0,  0,  0,  0,  0,  0,
  0,  0,  0,  0,  0,  0,  0,  0,
  0,  0,  0,  0,  0,  0,  0,  0,
  8,  6,  8,  0,  0,  0,  0,  0,
  8,10,  8,  0,  0,  0,  0,  0,
  0,  0,  0,  0,  0,  0,  0,  0
}
};
```

/* **kingside_defence** stores values for the pawn position if a king is on the kingside. There is a score for pawns being on the 2nd or 3rd rank. */

```
const int kingside_defence[2][64]=
{
{
  0,  0,  0,  0,  0,  0,  0,  0,
  0,  0,  0,  0,  0,  8,10,  8,
  0,  0,  0,  0,  0,  8,  6,  8,
  0,  0,  0,  0,  0,  0,  0,  0,
  0,  0,  0,  0,  0,  0,  0,  0,
  0,  0,  0,  0,  0,  0,  0,  0,
  8,  6,  8,  0,  0,  8,  8,  8,
  0,  0,  0,  0,  0,  0,  0,  0
},
{
  0,  0,  0,  0,  0,  0,  0,  0,
  0,  0,  0,  0,  0,  0,  0,  0,
  0,  0,  0,  0,  0,  0,  0,  0,
  0,  0,  0,  0,  0,  0,  0,  0,
  0,  0,  0,  0,  0,  0,  0,  0,
  0,  0,  0,  0,  0,  8,  6,  8,
  0,  0,  0,  0,  0,  8,10,  8,
  0,  0,  0,  0,  0,  0,  0,  0
}
};
```

Eval

/* **Eval()** is reasonably simple. It adds a score for each unit on the board.

If the unit is a pawn, it adds a score returned from **EvalPawn()**.

If the unit is a rook, it adds a score returned from **EvalRook()**.

It then adds a score for the king position, depending on whether the opponent has a queen. If the opponent has a queen, there is a bonus for having friendly pawns near the king. If the king is on the kingside, then the **kingside_pawns** score is used; otherwise the **queenside_pawns** score is used.

It returns the score of the side to move minus the opponent's score.

There are plenty of things that could be added to the eval function.
*/

```
int Eval()
{
  int score[2] = { 0,0 };
  memset(queenside_pawns, 0, sizeof(queenside_pawns));
  memset(kingside_pawns, 0, sizeof(kingside_pawns));
  BITBOARD b1;
  int sq;
  for (int x = 0; x < 2; x++)
  {
    b1 = bit_pieces[x][P];
    while (b1)
    {
      sq = NextBit(b1);
      b1 &= b1 - 1;
      score[x] += square_score[x][P][sq];
      score[x] += EvalPawn(x, sq);
    }
    b1 = bit_pieces[x][N];
    while (b1)
    {
      sq = NextBit(b1);
      b1 &= b1 - 1;
      score[x] += square_score[x][N][sq];
```

```
      }
      b1 = bit_pieces[x][B];
      while (b1)
      {
        sq = NextBit(b1);
        b1 &= b1 - 1;
        score[x] += square_score[x][B][sq];
      }
      b1 = bit_pieces[x][R];
      while (b1)
      {
        sq = NextBit(b1);
        b1 &= b1 - 1;
        score[x] += square_score[x][R][sq];
        score[x] += EvalRook(x, sq);
      }
      b1 = bit_pieces[x][Q];
      while (b1)
      {
        sq = NextBit(b1);
        b1 &= b1 - 1;
        score[x] += square_score[x][Q][sq];
      }
      if (bit_pieces[x ^ 1][Q] == 0)
        score[x] += king_endgame[x]
[NextBit(bit_pieces[x][K])];
      else
      {
        if (bit_pieces[x][K] & mask_kingside)
          score[x] += kingside_pawns[x];
        else if (bit_pieces[x][K] & mask_queenside)
          score[x] += queenside_pawns[x];
      }
   }
   return score[side] - score[xside];
}
```

EvalPawn

/* **EvalPawn()** evaluates each pawn and gives a bonus for *passed pawns* and a minus for *isolated pawns*. It also adds the kingside_pawns and queenside_pawns scores. */

```
static int EvalPawn(const int s, const int x)
{
   int score = 0;
```

```
  if (!(mask_passed[s][x] & bit_pieces[s ^ 1][P]) && !
(mask_path[s][x] & bit_pieces[s][P]))
    {
      score += passed[s][x];
    }
  if ((mask_isolated[x] & bit_pieces[s][P]) == 0)
      score -= ISOLATED;
  kingside_pawns[s] += kingside_defence[s][x];
  queenside_pawns[s] += queenside_defence[s][x];
  return score;
}
```

Passed Pawns

/* With bitboards, you can determine whether a pawn is passed or not with **one** if statement.

Firstly, you need to have an array of bitboards, which are initialised when the program starts. */

```
U64 passed[2][64];
```

/* Stores what squares need to be empty to show that a pawn on a certain square is passed. **bit_pieces[White][P]** and **bit_pieces[Black][P]** store what squares are occupied by pawns.

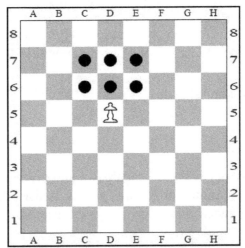

The white pawn is passed, provided there are no black pawns on any of the highlighted squares.

With white going up the board, **passed[White][D5]** looks like this.

```
0 0 0 0 0 0 0 0
0 0 1 1 1 0 0 0
0 0 1 1 1 0 0 0
0 0 0 0 0 0 0 0
0 0 0 0 0 0 0 0
0 0 0 0 0 0 0 0
0 0 0 0 0 0 0 0
0 0 0 0 0 0 0 0 */
```

```
if(!(bit_pieces[Black][P] & passed[White][D5))
```

/* then you know the white pawn on **d5** is passed.

Weak Pawns

An isolated pawn is a pawn with no friendly pawns on adjacent files. It is called weak because it cannot be defended by a pawn. It also cannot move and defend a friendly pawn.

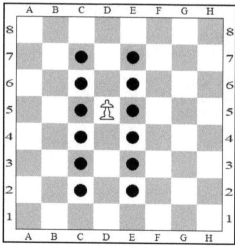

The white pawn is isolated, provided there are no white pawns on any of the highlighted squares. With white going up the board, **mask_isolated[White][D5]** looks like this.

```
0 0 0 0 0 0 0 0
0 0 1 0 1 0 0 0
0 0 1 0 1 0 0 0
0 0 1 0 1 0 0 0
0 0 1 0 1 0 0 0
0 0 1 0 1 0 0 0
0 0 1 0 1 0 0 0
0 0 0 0 0 0 0 0
```

You can also test whether a pawn is isolated or not with one statement. */

```
if((mask_isolated[x] & bit_pieces[s][P])==0)
  score -= ISOLATED;
```

EvalRook()

/* **EvalRook()** evaluates each rook and gives a bonus for being on a half-open file or an open file. A half-open file has no pawns of the same side on it. An open file has no pawns of either side. */

```
static int EvalRook(const int s, const int sq)
{
  int score = 0;
  if (!(mask_cols[sq] & bit_pieces[s][P]))
  {
    score = 10;
    if (!(mask_cols[sq] & bit_pieces[s ^ 1][P]))
      score = 20;
  }
  return score;
}
```

Search

Deepening iteration

This is a process in which:

- Starting from the root position, there is a search of 1 ply.
- Starting from the root position, there is a search of 2 ply.
- Starting from the root position, there is a search of 3 ply.
- etc.

The search continues until a **fixed depth** has been reached or the allotted time has been reached. When the search ends, the engine will play the best move it has found. This loop is in **think()**.

You may ask, why not do just one search to a great depth? Deepening iteration has some advantages. If time runs out, you will still be able to use the best move from the last iteration. More importantly, each iteration improves the sorting order of the moves. Sorting order is critical.

Move Ordering

The order in which candidate moves are searched makes a large difference.

A computer program that examines weakest moves first, that examines 1,000,000 positions, will need to examine approximately 500,000 positions if the moves are ordered randomly.

When the strongest moves are examined first, the number of positions is only 1,000. The optimum number is the square root of the least efficient ordering. This is a **massive** difference.

Chess programs go to a lot of trouble with their ordering of candidate moves.

The engine looks at moves in the following order.

1. The move from the hash table, if there is one.
2. Captures, sorted by most valuable captured, least valuable attacker.
3. History moves.
4. Other moves.

search.cpp

```
#include
#include "globals.h"
jmp_buf env;
bool stop_search;
int currentmax;
int root_start,root_dest;
```

think()

/* **think()** launches the search.

If the allotted time for the move runs out, program flow jumps to the line: */

```
setjmp(env);
```

/* and restores the game position and ends the search.

If a fixed time for each move has not been set, then the allotted time is halved for moves that are check evasions or likely recaptures.

The starting time is stored.

History tables are cleared.

It iterates until the maximum depth for the move is reached or until the allotted time has run out. Each iteration it calls **search()**. alpha is set low while beta is set high. **alpha** increases while **beta** decreases. **alpha** and **beta** move closer together.

The principal variation is then displayed using **printf** statements. This is the best line of play by both sides.

If the score is greater than 9000, it means a forced mate has been found, in which case it stops searching. */

```c
void think()
{
  int score;
  stop_search = false;
  setjmp(env);
  if (stop_search)
  {
    while (ply)
      UnMakeMove();
    return;
  }
  if (fixed_time == 0)
  {
    if (Attack(xside, NextBit(bit_pieces[side][K])))
      max_time = max_time / 2;
  }
  start_time = GetTime();
  stop_time = start_time + max_time;
  ply = 0;
  nodes = 0;
  NewPosition();
  memset(history, 0, sizeof(history));
  //printf("ply    nodes  score  pv\n");
  for (int i = 1; i <= max_depth; ++i)
  {
    currentmax = i;
    if (fixed_depth == 0 && max_depth > 1)
      if (fixed_time == 1)
      {
        if (GetTime() >= start_time + max_time)
        {
          stop_search = true;
          return;
        }
      }
      else if (GetTime() >= start_time + max_time / 4)
      {
        stop_search = true;
        return;
      }
```

```
    score = Search(-10000, 10000, i);
    printf("%d %d %d %d ", i, score, (GetTime() -
start_time) / 10, nodes);
    if (LookUp(side))
    {
      DisplayPV(i);
    }
    printf("\n");
    fflush(stdout);
    if (score > 9000 || score < -9000)
    {
      break;
    }
  }
}
```

Search()

/* **Search()** is the main part of the search.

- *alpha* is the best score the player has found so far.
- *beta* is the best score the opponent has found so far.
- *depth* is the number of **ply** to go before **max_ply** is reached.

*/

```
static int Search(int alpha, int beta, int depth)
{
  if (ply && Reps2())
  {
    return 0;
  }
```

/* If the position is repeated, we do not need to look any further. */

```
if (depth < 1)
    return CaptureSearch(alpha,beta);
```

/* If depth has run out, the capture search is done. */

```
  nodes++;
```

```
if ((nodes & 4095) == 0 && fixed_depth == 0)
{
  CheckUp();
}
```

/* Every 4,096 positions, the time is checked with CheckUp(). If time is low, program flow jumps out of Search(). */

```
if(ply > MAX_PLY-2)
   return Eval();
   if (ply > MAX_PLY-2)
     return Eval();
   int bestscore = -10001;
   int check = 0;
   if (Attack(xside, NextBit(bit_pieces[side][K])))
   {
     check = 1;
   }
   Gen(side, xside);
```

/* Moves are generated with **Gen()**. */

```
move_data bestmove = move_list[first_move[ply]];
   if (LookUp(side))
     SetHashMove();
   int count = 0;
   int score;
   int d;
   for (int i = first_move[ply]; i < first_move[ply +
1]; ++i)
   {
     Sort(i);
```

/* The moves are looped through **first_move[ply]** in order of their score. */

```
   if(!MakeMove(move_list[i]))
     continue;
```

/* If a move is illegal, then it is skipped over. For example, if the move attempts to move a pinned piece. */

```
count++;
  if (Attack(xside, NextBit(bit_pieces[side][K])))
  {
    d = depth;
  }
  else
  {
    d = depth - 3;
    if (move_list[i].flags & CAPTURE || count == 1
|| check == 1)
    {
      d = depth - 1;
    }
    else if (move_list[i].score > 0)
    {
      d = depth - 2;
    }
  }
```

/* If it is the move from the hash table, a capture or check evasion ,
then a normal search is done. This is done by subtracting 1 from
depth with **d = depth - 1**.

If the move is check, we **extend** by one ply. This is done by not
changing depth in the call to search with **d = depth**. A check
extension also prevents the search from entering capture search
when in check.

If it has a score greater than zero we **reduce** by one ply. This is
done by subtracting 2 from depth with **d = depth - 2**. Otherwise,
we **reduce** by two plies. This is done by subtracting 3 from depth.
*/

```
score = -Search(-beta, -alpha, d);
UnMakeMove();
```

/* The move is taken back with **TakeBack()**. */

```
if(score > bestscore)
{
  bestscore = score;
  bestmove = move_list[i];
```

```
        }
        if (score > alpha)
        {
          if (score >= beta)
          {
            if(!(mask[move_list[i].to] & bit_all))
              history[move_list[i].from][move_list[i].to] +=
depth;
              AddHash(side, move_list[i]);
            return beta;
          }
          alpha = score;
        }
}
```

/* If the score from search is greater than beta, a **beta cutoff**
happens. No need to search any more moves at this depth.
Otherwise, if the score is greater than alpha, alpha is increased. */

```
    if (count == 0)
    {
      if (Attack(xside,NextBit(bit_pieces[side][K])))
      {
        return -10000 + ply;
      }
      else
        return 0;
    }
```

/* If there were no legal moves, it is either checkmate or stalemate,
depending on whether the king is attacked or not. */

```
if (fifty >= 100)
    return 0;
```

/* If 100 plies have been played (including the moves actually
played) then this line leads to a draw by the 50-move rule. A score
of zero is returned. */

```
AddHash(side, bestmove);
```

/* The best move is added to the hash table with **AddHash()**. */

```
    return alpha;
}
```

CaptureSearch()

/* **CaptureSearch()** evaluates the position. If the score is greater than **alpha**, it tests for a **beta** cutoff. If the position is more than a queen less than alpha (the best score that side can do with a capture), it doesn't search any more.

Otherwise, it generates all captures and does a recapture search to see if material is won. If so, the material gain is added to the score.

It is basically checking to see if the side that has just moved has any pieces *en prise*. If so, it subtracts the value of the material it has lost from the evaluation score.

It's desirable to evaluate a *quiet* position. This is one in which the player has no pieces *en prise*. Even better would be a position with no tactics at all, though that is not practical. */

```
static int CaptureSearch(int alpha, int beta)
{
    nodes++;
    int x = Eval();
    if (x > alpha)
    {
        if (x >= beta)
        {
            return beta;
        }
        alpha = x;
    }
    else if (x + piece_value[Q] < alpha)
        return alpha;
    int score = 0, bestmove = 0;
    int best = 0;
    GenCaptures(side, xside);
    for (int i = first_move[ply]; i < first_move[ply +
1]; ++i)
```

```
{
  Sort(i);
  if (x + piece_value[board[move_list[i].to]] <
alpha)
    {
      continue;
    }
  score = ReCaptureSearch(move_list[i].from,
move_list[i].to);
  if (score > best)
    {
      best = score;
      bestmove = i;
    }
  }
  if (best > 0)
  {
    x += best;
  }
  if (x > alpha)
  {
    if (x >= beta)
    {
      if (best > 0)
        AddHash(side, move_list[bestmove]);
      return beta;
    }
    return x;
  }
  return alpha;
}
```

ReCaptureSearch

/* **ReCaptureSearch()** searches the outcome of capturing and recapturing on the same square.

It stops searching if the value of the capturing piece is more than that of the captured piece and the next attacker.

For example, a White queen could take a rook, but a bishop could take the queen.

Even if White could take the bishop, it's not worth exchanging a queen for a rook and bishop.

MakeRecapture() detects pinned pieces. */

```
static int ReCaptureSearch(int a, const int sq)
{
    int b;
    int c = 0;
    int t = 0;
    int score[12];
    score[0] = piece_value[board[sq]];
    score[1] = piece_value[board[a]];
    int total_score = 0;
    while (c < 10)
    {
        if (!MakeRecapture(a, sq))
            break;
        t++;
        nodes++;
        c++;
        b = LowestAttacker(side, sq);
        if (b > -1)
        {
            score[c + 1] = piece_value[board[b]];
            if (score[c] > score[c - 1] + score[c + 1])
            {
                c--;
                break;
            }
        }
        else
        {
            break;
        }
        a = b;
    }
    while (c > 1)
    {
        if (score[c - 1] >= score[c - 2])
            c -= 2;
        else
            break;
    }
    for (int x = 0; x < c; x++)
    {
        if (x % 2 == 0)
```

```
      total_score += score[x];
    else
      total_score -= score[x];
  }
  while (t)
  {
    UnMakeRecapture();
    t--;
  }
  return total_score;
}
```

Reps2()

/* **Reps2()** searches backwards for an identical position. Positions are identical if the key and lock are the same, and it's the same player to move. The key is represented by **currentkey**, while the lock is represented by **currentlock**.

fifty represents the number of moves made since the last pawn move or capture. It compares the current position with the position 4 ply ago and tests if they are identical. If they are, the engine stops searching the last move and searches the next move. */

```
static int Reps2()
{
  for (int i = hply - 4; i >= hply - fifty; i -= 2)
  {
    if (i < 4)
      return 0;
    if (game_list[i].hash == currentkey &&
game_list[i].lock == currentlock)
      return 1;
  }
  return 0;
}
```

Sort()

/* **Sort()** searches the move list, starting after the last move searched for the move with the highest score.

The highest scoring move is moved to the top of the list so that it will be searched next. */

```
static void Sort(const int from)
{
  int best_score = move_list[from].score;
  int best_move = from;
  for (int i = from + 1; i < first_move[ply + 1]; i++)
    if (move_list[i].score > best_score)
    {
      best_score = move_list[i].score;
      best_move = i;
    }
  move_data g = move_list[from];
  move_list[from] = move_list[best_move];
  move_list[best_move] = g;
}
```

CheckUp()

/* **CheckUp()** checks to see if the time for the current move has run out. If so, the search ends.

It uses an unusual library function called **longjmp**, which is like **goto** except it branches to a label within a different function. */

```
static void CheckUp()
{
  if ((GetTime() >= stop_time || (max_time < 50 && ply
> 1)) && fixed_depth == 0 && ply > 1)
    stop_search = true;
  longjmp(env, 0);
}
```

SetHashMove()

/* **SetHashMove()** searches the move list for the move from the Hash Table. If it finds it, it gives the move a high score so that it will be played first. It also removes any possibility that the move from the hash table is illegal, due to a collision. */

```
static void SetHashMove()
{
  for (int x = first_move[ply]; x < first_move[ply +
1]; x++)
```

```
    {
      if (move_list[x].from == hash_move.from &&
move_list[x].to == hash_move.to)
        {
          move_list[x].score = HASH_SCORE;
          return;
        }
    }
}
```

DisplayPV

/* **DisplayPV** displays the principal variation(PV). This is the best line of play by both sides.

Firstly, it displays the best move at the root. This is the move that will eventually be played. It plays this move so that the current hash key and lock will be correct.

It looks up the Hash Table and finds the best move at the greater depth and continues until no more best moves can be found.

Lastly, it takes back the moves, returning to the original position. */

```
static void DisplayPV(int i)
{
  root_move = hash_move;
  for (int x = 0; x < i; x++)
  {
    if (LookUp(side) == false)
      break;
    printf(" ");
    Alg(hash_move.from, hash_move.to);
    MakeMove(hash_move);
  }
  while (ply)
    UnMakeMove();
}
```

hash.cpp

Transposition tables or hash tables for short, are very useful.

They store a single number representing the position.

Positions that caused a **beta cutoff** (i.e. the best move with current information) are stored in the hash table, along with the best move.

When a node is being searched, the hash table can be looked up. If the position has been searched before, the move in the hash table can be used first.

If the move caused a cutoff at a lower depth, then there is a good chance it will cause a cutoff again. This will save lots of time, as there is no need to search the remaining moves.

Note that for positions to be identical, it must be the same side to move in each case. There are different hash tables for positions in which it is white's move and for those in which it is black to move.

If the move in the hash table is illegal because it is an impossible *en passant* or castling, then it will be ignored.

```
hashp *hashpos[2];
unsigned int  hashpositions[2];
```

/* Pointers to **hashpos** are used so that the array size can be dynamically changed.

The pointers need to be freed when the program quits to return memory to the system.

Generally, the larger the hash table, the better.

Displaying the Principal Variation

The hash tables are very useful for displaying the **principal variation**. This is the best line of play by both sides.

- Start at the root position.
- Find the best move from the hash table.
- Make the move.
- Display the move.
- Continue these 3 steps until the position cannot be found in the hash table.
- Return to the root position.

Playing the Move

To find the move selected by the engine, look up the hash table.

Keys and Locks

```
*/

U64 hash[2][6][64];
U64 lock[2][6][64];
```

/* They both work in the same way. They are initialised with random values. There is a number for each type of piece for each square.

Current Key and Current Lock

```
*/

U64 currentkey,currentlock;
```

/* These store a number for the current position. They are updated whenever the position changes. This is much faster than continually recalculating keys for the entire board.

The current position can be looked up in the hash table.

AddKey() updates the currentkey and currentlock.

Collisions

A collision happens when different positions share the same key.
This is quite frequent, especially with smaller tables.

To reduce the number of collisions, a lock is used as well. The
chance of different positions having the same key and the same
lock is very low indeed. If there is a collision, then **AddHash()**
overwrites the current entry.

The fewer the number of collisions, the more efficient the hash
table is.

The larger the hash tables, the fewer collisions there will be. */

```
U64 collisions;
#include "globals.h"
BITBOARD hash[2][6][64];
BITBOARD lock[2][6][64];
BITBOARD currentkey,currentlock;
BITBOARD collisions;
static const BITBOARD MAXHASH =  5000000;
static const BITBOARD HASHSIZE = 5000000;
move_data hash_move;
struct hashp
{
  U64 hashlock;
  int from;
  int to;
  int flags;
};
hashp *hashpos[2];
```

RandomizeHash()

/* RandomizeHash() is called when the engine is started. The
whitehash, blackhash, whitelock and blacklock tables are filled
with random numbers. */

```
void RandomizeHash()
{
  for (int piece = 0; piece < 6; piece++)
    for (int x = 0; x < 64; x++)
    {
      hash[White][piece][x] = Random(HASHSIZE);
      hash[Black][piece][x] = Random(HASHSIZE);
      lock[White][piece][x] = Random(HASHSIZE);
      lock[Black][piece][x] = Random(HASHSIZE);
    }
  hashpos[0] = new hashp[MAXHASH];
  hashpos[1] = new hashp[MAXHASH];
}
```

Random()

/* **Random()** generates a random number up to the size of x. */

```
int Random(const int x)
{
  return rand() % x;
}
```

Free()

/* **Free()** Frees memory that was allocated to the hashpos pointers with **new**. */

```
void Free()
{
  delete hashpos[0];
  delete hashpos[1];
}
```

AddHash()

/* **AddHash()** adds an entry into the HashTable. The move is added, plus the current lock. The current key is the index of the table, so it does not need to be added. If that index is already being used, it simply overwrites it. */

```
void AddHash(const int s, const move_data m)
{
  hashp* ptr = &hashpos[s][currentkey];
  ptr->hashlock = currentlock;
  ptr->from = m.from;
  ptr->to = m.to;
  ptr->flags = m.flags;
}
```

AddKey()

/* **AddKey()** updates the current key and lock.

The key is a single number representing a position. Different positions may map to the same key.

The lock is very similar to the key (it's a second key), which is a different number because it was seeded with different random numbers.

While the odds of several positions having the same key are very high, the odds of two positions having the same key and the same lock are very, very low. */

```
void AddKey(const int s, const int piece, const int sq)
{
  currentkey ^= hash[s][piece][sq];
  currentlock ^= lock[s][piece][sq];
}
```

GetLock()

/* **GetLock()** gets the current lock from a position. This is only used when a game starts or a **fen** file is loaded. */

```
U64 GetLock()
{
  U64 loc = 0;
  for (int x = 0; x < 64; x++)
  {
    if (board[x] != EMPTY)
```

110

```
    {
      if (bit_units[White] & mask[x])
        loc ^= lock[White][board[x]][x];
      if (bit_units[Black] & mask[x])
        loc ^= lock[Black][board[x]][x];
    }
  }
  return loc;
}
```

GetKey()

/* **GetKey()** gets the current key from a position. This is only used when a game starts or a **fen** file is loaded. */

```
U64 GetKey()
{
  U64 key = 0;
  for (int x = 0; x < 64; x++)
  {
    if (board[x] != EMPTY)
    {
      if (bit_units[White] & mask[x])
        key ^= hash[White][board[x]][x];
      if (bit_units[Black] & mask[x])
        key ^= hash[Black][board[x]][x];
    }
  }
  return key;
}
```

LookUp()

/* **LookUp()** looks up the current position to see if it is in the HashTable. If so, it fetches the move stored there and returns **true**. If hashlock and currentlock don't match, it means there are 2 different positions with the same key, i.e. a collision. */

```
bool LookUp(const int s)
{
  if (hashpos[s][currentkey].hashlock != currentlock)
  {
    collisions++;
    return false;
  }
  hash_move.from = hashpos[s][currentkey].from;
  hash_move.to = hashpos[s][currentkey].to;
  hash_move.flags = hashpos[s][currentkey].flags;
  return true;
}
```

main.cpp

```cpp
#include "globals.h"
int flip = 0;
int computer_side;
int player[2];
int fixed_time;
int fixed_depth;
int max_time;
int start_time;
int stop_time;
int max_depth;
int turn = 0;
```

main()

/* **main()** displays program information and enters the main loop. The user enters commands and presses the Enter key. What is typed is read by **scanf()**. **strcmp** is used to respond to the command.

If no commands match and it is a human's turn, the command is parsed to see if it is a legal move.

This is an infinite loop until *xboard* or *quit* is entered.

You can play against the engine. However, to play other engines, the **xboard** function is called. */

```cpp
int main()
{
  cout << "Bills Bitboard Chess Engine" << endl;
  cout << "Version 1.1, 23/4/21" << endl;
  cout << "Bill Jordan 2021" << endl;
  cout << "FIDE Master and 2021 state champion." <<
endl;
  cout << "I have published many chess books" << endl;
  cout << "including books on chess programming." <<
endl;
  cout << "My author page at Amazon is at
billjordanchess" << endl;
```

```
  cout << "https://www.amazon.com/-/e/B07F5WSFHZ"  <<
endl;
  cout << endl;
  cout << "typing help displays a list of commands."
<< endl;
  cout << endl;
  string s;
  string sFen;
  string sText;
  int m;
  int turns = 0;
  int t;
  int lookup;
  double nps;
  fixed_time = 0;
  SetBits();
  SetUp();
  cout << "Engine loaded." << endl;
  side = 0;//
  while (true)
  {
    if (side == computer_side)
    {
      think();
      turns++;
      currentkey = GetKey();
      currentlock = GetLock();
      cout << endl << "Computer's move: ";
      Alg(root_move.from, root_move.to); cout << endl;
      cout << "Collisions " << collisions < 0)
        nps = (double)nodes / (double)t;
      else
        nps = 0;
      nps *= 1000.0;
      cout << endl << "Nodes per second: " << (int)nps
<< endl;
      ply = 0;
      first_move[0] = 0;
      Gen(side,xside);
      PostResult();
      cout << "Turn " << ++turn << endl;
      DisplayBoard();
      continue;
    }
    cout << "Enter move or command> ";
    cin >> s;
    if (s == "d")
```

```
{
  DisplayBoard();
  continue;
}
if (s == "f")
{
  flip = 1 - flip;
  DisplayBoard();
  continue;
}
if (s == "go")
{
  computer_side = side;
  continue;
}
if (s == "help")
{
  ShowHelp();
  continue;
}
if (s == "moves")
{
  cout << "Moves" << endl;
  for (int i = 0; i < first_move[1]; ++i)
  {
    Alg(move_list[i].from, move_list[i].to);
  }
  continue;
}
if (s =="new")
{
  NewGame();
  computer_side = EMPTY;
  continue;
}
if (s == "on" || s == "p")
{
  computer_side = side;
  continue;
}
if (s =="off")
{
  computer_side = EMPTY;
  continue;
}
if (s =="quit")
{
```

```
      cout << "Program exiting" << endl;
      break;
   }
   if (s == "sb")
   {
      sFen ="c:\\diagrams\\";//You will need to
replace this with the folder you use for your
diagrams.
      cin >> sText;
      sFen += sText + ".fen";
      LoadDiagram(sFen);
      continue;
   }
   if (s == "sd")
   {
     cin >> max_depth;
     max_time = 1 << 25;
     fixed_depth = 1;
     continue;
   }
   if (s == "st")
   {
     cin >> max_time;
     max_time *= 1000;
     max_depth = MAX_PLY;
     fixed_time = 1;
     continue;
   }
   if (s == "sw")
   {
     side = 1 - side;
     xside = 1 - xside;
     continue;
   }
   if (s == "undo")
   {
     if (!hply)
       continue;
     computer_side = EMPTY;
     UnMakeMove();
     ply = 0;
     if (first_move[0] != 0)
       first_move[0] = 0;
     Gen(side, xside);
     continue;
   }
   if (s == "xboard")
```

```
    {
      xboard();
      break;
    }
    ply = 0;
    first_move[0] = 0;
    Gen(side, xside);
    m = ParseMove(s);
    if (m == -1 || !MakeMove(move_list[m]))
    {
      cout << "Illegal move." << endl;
      cout << s << endl;
      MoveString(move_list[m].from, move_list[m].to,
0);
      if (m == -1)
        cout << " m = -1"  << endl;
    }
    if (game_list[hply].flags & PROMOTE &&
(row[move_list[m].to] == 0 || row[move_list[m].to] ==
7))
    {
      RemovePiece(xside, Q, move_list[m].to);
      if (s[4] == 'n' || s[4] == 'N')
        AddPiece(xside, N, move_list[m].to);
      else if (s[4] == 'b' || s[4] == 'B')
        AddPiece(xside, B, move_list[m].to);
      else if (s[4] == 'r' || s[4] == 'r')
        AddPiece(xside, R, move_list[m].to);
      else AddPiece(xside, Q, move_list[m].to);
    }
  }
  Free();
  return 0;
}
```

ParseMove()

/* **ParseMove()** parses the move and sees if it matches a legal move in the move list. The move is expected to be in the form e2e4 (i.e. **from square** followed by the **to square**). The letters a-h are converted to digits representing the file and rank. The file and rank are converted to a square. If there is no match, it returns -1. */

```
static int ParseMove(string s)
{
  int from, to, i;
  if (s[0] < 'a' || s[0] > 'h' ||
    s[1] < '0' || s[1] > '9' ||
    s[2] < 'a' || s[2] > 'h' ||
    s[3] < '0' || s[3] > '9')
    return -1;
  from = s[0] - 'a';
  from += ((s[1] - '0') - 1) * 8;
  to = s[2] - 'a';
  to += ((s[3] - '0') - 1) * 8;
  for (i = 0; i < first_move[1]; ++i)
    if (move_list[i].from == from && move_list[i].to
== to)
    {
      if (s[4] == 'n' || s[4] == 'N')
        move_list[i].flags |= PROMOTE_KNIGHT;
      if (s[4] == 'b' || s[4] == 'B')
        move_list[i].flags |= PROMOTE_BISHOP;
      else if (s[4] == 'r' || s[4] == 'R')
        move_list[i].flags |= PROMOTE_BISHOP;
      return i;
    }
  return -1;
}
```

DisplayBoard

/* **DisplayBoard()** displays the board. The windows.h header file is needed, so that the Console object can be used. This allows the position to be displayed in colour. */

```
void DisplayBoard()
{
  HANDLE hConsole;
  hConsole = GetStdHandle(STD_OUTPUT_HANDLE);
  int text = 15;
  int i;
  int x = 0;
  int c;
  if (flip == 0)
    cout << "\n8";
  else
    cout << "\n1";
  for (int j = 0; j < 64; ++j)
```

```
{
  if (flip == 0)
    i = Flip[j];
  else
    i = 63 - Flip[j];
  c = 6;
  if (bit_units[White] & mask[i]) c = 0;
  if (bit_units[Black] & mask[i]) c = 1;
  switch (c)
  {
  case EMPTY:
    if (board_color[i] == 0)
      text = 127;
    else
      text = 34;
    SetConsoleTextAttribute(hConsole, text);
    cout << " ";
    SetConsoleTextAttribute(hConsole, 15);
    break;
  case 0:
    if (board_color[i] == 0)
      text = 126;
    else
      text = 46;
    SetConsoleTextAttribute(hConsole, text);
    cout << " " << piece_char[c][board[i]];
    SetConsoleTextAttribute(hConsole, 15);
    break;
  case 1:
    if (board_color[i] == 0)
      text = 112;
    else
      text = 32;
    SetConsoleTextAttribute(hConsole, text);
    cout << " " << piece_char[c][board[i]];
    SetConsoleTextAttribute(hConsole, 15);
    break;
  default:
    cout << " ." << c;
    break;
  }
  if ((bit_all & mask[i]) && board[i] == EMPTY)
    if (x == 0)
      cout << " " << c;
    else
      cout << " ";
  if (board[i] < 0 || board[i] > 6)
```

```
    if (x == 0)
      cout << " ." << board[i];
    else
      cout << "  " << board[i];
  if (flip == 0)
  {
    if ((j + 1) % 8 == 0 && j != 63)
      cout << endl << row[i];
  }
  else
  {
    if ((j + 1) % 8 == 0 && row[i] != 7)
      cout << endl << row[j] + 2;
  }
 }
 if (flip == 0)
   cout << "\n\n    a b c d e f g h\n\n";
 else
   cout << "\n\n    h g f e d c b a\n\n";
}
```

xboard()

/* **xboard()** is similar to **main()** except that it is designed for commands sent to and from Winboard, which connects the engine with another engine. This enables the engine to use graphics of a program like Arena. */

```
static void xboard()
{
  int computer_side;
  char line[256], command[256];
  int m;
  int analyze = 0;
  int lookup;
  signal(SIGINT, SIG_IGN);
  printf("\n");
  NewGame();
  fixed_time = 0;
  computer_side = EMPTY;
  while (true)
  {
    fflush(stdout);
    if (side == computer_side)
    {
      think();
```

```
   SetMaterial();
   Gen(side, xside);
   currentkey = GetKey();
   currentlock = GetLock();
   lookup = LookUp(side);
   if (root_move.from != 0 || root_move.to != 0)
   {
     hash_move.from = root_move.from;
     hash_move.to = root_move.to;
   }
   else
     printf(" lookup=0 ");
   move_list[0].from = hash_move.from;
   move_list[0].to = hash_move.to;
   printf("move %s\n", MoveString(hash_move.from,
hash_move.to, hash_move.flags));
   MakeMove(hash_move);
   ply = 0;
   Gen(side, xside);
   PostResult();
   continue;
 }
 if (!fgets(line, 256, stdin))
   return;
 if (line[0] == '\n')
   continue;
 sscanf(line, "%s", command);
 if (!strcmp(command, "xboard"))
   continue;
 if (!strcmp(command, "new"))
 {
   NewGame();
   computer_side = 1;
   continue;
 }
 if (!strcmp(command, "quit"))
   return;
 if (!strcmp(command, "force"))
 {
   computer_side = EMPTY;
   continue;
 }
 if (!strcmp(command, "white"))
 {
   side = 0;
   xside = 1;
   Gen(side, xside);
```

```
    computer_side = 1;
    continue;
}
if (!strcmp(command, "black"))
{
    side = 1;
    xside = 0;
    Gen(side, xside);
    computer_side = 0;
    continue;
}
if (!strcmp(command, "st"))
{
    sscanf_s(line, "st %d", &max_time);
    max_time *= 1000;
    max_depth = MAX_PLY;
    fixed_time = 1;
    continue;
}
if (!strcmp(command, "sd"))
{
    sscanf_s(line, "sd %d", &max_depth);
    max_time = 1 << 25;
    continue;
}
if (!strcmp(command, "time"))
{
    sscanf_s(line, "time %d", &max_time);
    if (max_time < 200)
        max_depth = 1;
    else
    {
        max_time /= 2;
        max_depth = MAX_PLY;
    }
    continue;
}
if (!strcmp(command, "otim"))
{
    continue;
}
if (!strcmp(command, "go"))
{
    computer_side = side;
    continue;
}
if (!strcmp(command, "random"))
```

```
      continue;
    if (!strcmp(command, "level"))
      continue;
    if (!strcmp(command, "hard"))
      continue;
    if (!strcmp(command, "easy"))
      continue;
    if (!strcmp(command, "hint"))
    {
      think();
      currentkey = GetKey();
      currentlock = GetLock();
      lookup = LookUp(side);
      if (hash_move.from == 0 && hash_move.to == 0)
        continue;
      printf("Hint: %s\n", MoveString(hash_move.from,
hash_move.to, 0));
      continue;
    }
    if (!strcmp(command, "undo"))
    {
      if (!hply)
        continue;
      UnMakeMove();
      ply = 0;
      Gen(side, xside);
      continue;
    }
    if (!strcmp(command, "remove"))
    {
      if (hply < 2)
        continue;
      UnMakeMove();
      UnMakeMove();
      ply = 0;
      Gen(side, xside);
      continue;
    }
    first_move[0] = 0;
    Gen(side, xside);
    m = ParseMove(line);
    if (m == -1 || !MakeMove(move_list[m]))
      printf("Error (unknown command): %s\n",
command);
    else
    {
      ply = 0;
```

```
      Gen(side, xside);
      PostResult();
    }
  }
}
```

PostResult()

/* **PostResult()** checks to see if the end of the game has been reached.

Firstly, it checks to see if either side has mating material. If not, the game is drawn. It prints *1/2-1/2 {Stalemate}\n* because that is what Winboard recognises.

Next, it sees if there are any legal moves and sees whether it's checkmate or stalemate.

It then checks for draws by repetition or the fifty-move rule. */

```
static void PostResult()
{
  int i;
  int flag = 0;
  SetMaterial();
  Gen(side, xside);
  for (i = 0; i < first_move[1]; ++i)
    if (MakeMove(move_list[i]))
    {
      UnMakeMove();
      flag = 1;
      break;
    }
  if (pawn_mat[White] == 0 && pawn_mat[Black] == 0 &&
    piece_mat[White] <= piece_value[N] &&
piece_mat[Black] <= piece_value[N])
  {
    printf("1/2-1/2 {Stalemate}\n");
    NewGame();
    computer_side = EMPTY;
    return;
  }
  if (i == first_move[1] && flag == 0)
  {
```

```
    Gen(side, xside);
    DisplayBoard();
    printf(" end of game_data ");
    if (Attack(xside, NextBit(bit_pieces[side][K])))
    {
      if (side == 0)
      {
        printf("0-1 {Black mates}\n");
      }
      else
      {
        printf("1-0 {White mates}\n");
      }
    }
    else
    {
      printf("1/2-1/2 {Stalemate}\n");
    }
    NewGame();
    computer_side = EMPTY;
  }
  else if (Reps() >= 3)
  {
    printf("1/2-1/2 {Draw by repetition}\n");
    NewGame();
    computer_side = EMPTY;
  }
  else if (fifty >= 100)
  {
    printf("1/2-1/2 {Draw by fifty move rule}\n");
    NewGame();
    computer_side = EMPTY;
  }
}
```

Reps()

/* **Reps()** checks for repetition by the moves actually played (not in a search). It does this by comparing the current key and lock with previous keys and locks. */

```
static int Reps()
{
  int r = 0;
  for (int i = hply; i >= hply - fifty; i -= 2)
    if (game_list[i].hash == currentkey &&
```

```
game_list[i].lock == currentlock)
      r++;
  return r;
}
```

LoadDiagram()

/* **LoadDiagram()** loads a position from a fen file. A fen file includes the board position, the side to move and the castling permissions for both sides. The engine can play moves from this position. The fen string is parsed, and the board is set up. */

```
static int LoadDiagram(string file_name)
{
  ifstream file(file_name);
  if (!file) {
    cerr << "File not found!" << endl;
    return 1;
  }
  string fen_text;
  getline(file, fen_text);
  int x, n = 0;
  int c = 0, i = 0, j;
  memset(pawn_mat, 0, sizeof(pawn_mat));
  memset(piece_mat, 0, sizeof(piece_mat));
  memset(bit_pieces, 0, sizeof(bit_pieces));
  memset(bit_units, 0, sizeof(bit_units));
  bit_all = 0;
    for (x = 0; x < 64; x++)
    {
      board[x] = EMPTY;
    }
    while (fen_text[c])
    {
      if (fen_text[c] >= '0' && fen_text[c] <= '8')
        i += fen_text[c] - 48;
      if (fen_text[c] == '\\')
        continue;
      j = Flip[i];
      switch (fen_text[c])
      {
      case 'K': AddPiece(0, K, j); i++; break;
      case 'Q': AddPiece(0, Q, j); i++; break;
      case 'R': AddPiece(0, R, j); i++; break;
      case 'B': AddPiece(0, B, j); i++; break;
      case 'N': AddPiece(0, N, j); i++; break;
```

```
        case 'P': AddPiece(0, P, j); i++; break;
        case 'k': AddPiece(1, K, j); i++; break;
        case 'q': AddPiece(1, Q, j); i++; break;
        case 'r': AddPiece(1, R, j); i++; break;
        case 'b': AddPiece(1, B, j); i++; break;
        case 'n': AddPiece(1, N, j); i++; break;
        case 'p': AddPiece(1, P, j); i++; break;
        }
        c++;
        if (fen_text[c] == ' ')
          break;
        if (i > 63)
          break;
      }
      if (fen_text[c] == ' ' && fen_text[c + 2] == ' ')
      {
        if (fen_text[c + 1] == 'w')
        {
          side = 0; xside = 1;
        }
        if (fen_text[c + 1] == 'b')
        {
          side = 1; xside = 0;
        }
      }
    }
castle = 0;
while (fen_text[c])
{
  switch (fen_text[c])
  {
  case '-': break;
  case 'K':if (bit_pieces[White][K] & mask[E1]) castle
|= CASTLE_G1;
    break;
  case 'Q':if (bit_pieces[White][K] & mask[E1]) castle
|= CASTLE_C1;
    break;
  case 'k':if (bit_pieces[Black][K] & mask[E8]) castle
|= CASTLE_G8;
    break;
  case 'q':if (bit_pieces[Black][K] & mask[E8]) castle
|= CASTLE_C8;
    break;
  default: break;
  }
  c++;
}
```

```
NewPosition();
DisplayBoard();
Gen(side, xside);
if (side == 0)
  cout << "White to move" << endl;
else
  cout << "Black to move" << endl;
cout << fen_text << endl;
return 0;
}
```

ShowHelp()

/* **ShowHelp()** displays help on the different commands. */

```
static void ShowHelp()
{
  cout << "d - Displays the board." << endl;
  cout << "f - Flips the board." << endl;
  cout << "go - Starts the engine." << endl;
  cout << "help - Displays help on the commands." <<
endl;
  cout << "moves - Displays a list of possible moves."
<< endl;
  cout << "new - Starts a new game_data ." << endl;
  cout << "off - Turns the computer player off." <<
endl;
  cout << "on or p - The computer plays a move." <<
endl;
  cout << "sb - Loads a fen diagram." << endl;
  cout << "sd - Sets the search depth." << endl;
  cout << "st - Sets the time limit per move in
seconds." << endl;
  cout << "sw - Switches sides." << endl;
  cout << "quit - Quits the program." << endl;
  cout << "undo - Takes back the last move." << endl;
  cout << "xboard - Starts xboard." << endl;
}
```

SetUp()

/* **SetUp()** performs some initialisation before the main loop starts.
*/

```
void SetUp()
{
  RandomizeHash();
  SetTables();
  SetMoves();
  InitBoard();
  computer_side = EMPTY;
  max_time = 1 << 25;
  max_depth = 8;
}
```

/* **max_depth** is set to an arbitrary value of 4.

NewGame()

NewGame() performs some initialisation before a game starts. */

```
void NewGame()
{
  InitBoard();
  Gen(side, xside);
}
```

SetMaterial()

/* **SetMaterial()** calculates the pawn and piece scores for both sides. This is used to detect draws by insufficient mating material. */

```
void SetMaterial()
{
  int color;
  memset(pawn_mat, 0, sizeof(pawn_mat));
  memset(piece_mat, 0, sizeof(piece_mat));
  for (int x = 0; x < 64; x++)
  {
    if (board[x] != EMPTY)
    {
      if (bit_units[White] & mask[x])
        color = 0;
      else
        color = 1;
      if (board[x] == P)
        pawn_mat[color] += piece_value[P];
```

```
    else
      piece_mat[color] += piece_value[board[x]];
    }
  }
}
```

GetTime()

/* **GetTime()** gets the system time. */

```
int GetTime()
{
  struct timeb timebuffer;
  ftime(&timebuffer);
  return (timebuffer.time * 1000) +
timebuffer.millitm;
}
```

MoveString()

/* **MoveString()** converts a move to a string. */

```
static string MoveString(int from, int to, int
promote)
{
  string str = "";
  str += (col[from] + 'a');
  str += (row[from] + 1);
  str += (col[to] + 'a');
  str += (row[to] + 1);
  string promote_piece[] =
{ "-","n","b","r","q","q" };
  if (promote > 0)
  {
    str += promote_piece[promote];
  }
  return str;
}
```

I originally used the free 2010 Microsoft Visual C++ Express compiler, and now use Visual Studio 2019. The project is a Win32 console application.

Project

This project consists of 8 .cpp files and one header file.

These are:

- globals.h
- attack.cpp
- bitboard.cpp
- eval.cpp
- gen.cpp
- hash.cpp
- init.cpp
- main.cpp
- search.cpp
- update.cpp

Creating an executable chess program

1. Download and install the free Microsoft Visual C++ 2010 program.
2. Go to <u>my github page</u>.
3. Go to <u>releases</u>.
4. Download and extract the compressed **bitboard.chess1.1.rar** file.
5. Find the **bitboard chess.sln** file.
6. Run this, and it will load the project in Visual C++.
7. Build and run the program.
8. There are likely a few warnings related to scanf; however, these are not critical.

An alternative is to download the **bitboard.chess1.1.exe** file.

This can be run with Arena, Winboard or any chess interface that supports Winboard engines.

You can run the program with Arena using the following steps:

- Download and install the free Arena program.
- Start Arena.
- Select **Install new engine** from the **Engines** menu.
- Select the engine.exe (or whatever you have renamed it to) from the Dialogue box.
- Select **Winboard** in the **Select the type of Engine** dialogue. Click OK.
- Click NO to start the engine, unless you want to start it.
- Select **Manage** from the **Engines** menu.
- Select the engine.exe and click on details.
- Here you can edit the author and country fields, add an opening book, etc.
- You can now run tournaments with the newly installed engine. You can create separate versions of it and have it

play itself.

It can also be run with the original Winboard program. Note that it is a Winboard engine, not a UCI engine.

Tinkering

There are plenty of ways of tinkering with the code. You can alter the code, compile it and see how it goes. You can play the engine against different versions of itself.

Profiler

A useful tool which can be used with this compiler is the freely downloadable *Very Sleepy* profiler. You run **Very Sleepy**, launch an .exe file, run it for a few moments and see the results.

You can see what percentage of execution time is spent by each function. It can highlight bottlenecks in your code that you may have been unaware of.

Profiling *Bitboard Chess 1.0* showed that the function that used the most time was **Eval()**. This information shows that finding ways to make Eval() faster would be very useful.

Possible Improvements

How to make the engine stronger.

Engines can be made stronger by:

- Increasing speed or **nps** (nodes per second).
- Improving search.
- Improving evaluation.
- Improving time management and other practical play factors.

There is a myriad of ways in which the engine can be improved. The challenge is how to improve it without losing too much speed.

Evaluation

The evaluation is very fast, but crude.

Search

The *branching factor* is very high; sometimes a *tree explosion* happens. The branching factor is the number of nodes searched on the last iteration relative to the total number of nodes. Doubling each time would be a good branching factor. Increasing tenfold or more each iteration is a disaster.

Pawn Hash Tables

Pawn hash tables greatly increase the speed of this engine. This is because often different positions have the same pawn position as positions that have been searched before. In those cases, rather than evaluating the pawn structure each time, you simply look up the pawn hash table and retrieve the score. It's even better for games in which there are mostly blocked pawns.

Pawn hash tables can be much smaller than normal hash tables.

They use locks and keys, which are updated and used in a similar manner as standard hash tables.

Incremental Evaluation

Looping through the board to find pieces is very slow. It's quicker to use the piece material and square scores from the previous position. These can be updated as pieces are made and unmade.

Opening Book

An effective way to implement an opening book is to prefill the hash table with opening positions, plus a move to play from each position. Storing positions is better than storing just moves, as that way, opening transpositions can be detected.

Preferably, you need a process by which you read a pgn file with many games and fill up the opening book. I have done it, but it takes some time.

Alpha Zero and Leela Zero

An exciting development in recent years has been the development of several strong new engines combining neural networks with a Monte Carlo Tree Search. This topic is covered in my book *How to Write a Simple Chess Neural Network.*

Acknowledgements

Over the years, I have looked at the source code of other chess engines for inspiration. Some of the engines I have looked at and used ideas for this engine include:

- Crafty
- GNUChess
- TSCP
- CPW
- Stockfish
- and others.

Some code from TSCP was useful for the Winboard commands.

Where to go from here?

I hope you have enjoyed my book. I suggest that after finishing it, you re-read it after several weeks. You may grasp points that were previously obscure to you.

It is easy for me to make small changes and update this book. If you have any constructive suggestions, you can email me at **swneerava@gmail.com**. Feel welcome to suggest topics for a Chess book you would like to see written. Positive reviews are welcome.

About the Author

Bill Jordan was taught chess on his 7th birthday by his father, using a chess set carved by his grandfather. Four years later, he started reading chess books. Four years later, he became Victorian Junior chess champion.

He later became Australian junior chess champion, Victorian chess champion, Australian correspondence chess champion, South Australian chess champion and Australian senior champion. Since the age of 17 Bill Jordan has represented Australia in international chess events in Malaysia, Yugoslavia, Mexico and China.

Since 1981, Bill has been a life member and has been president of the Melbourne chess club, one of the oldest chess clubs in the world.

He is an enthusiastic chess software programmer who has taught and written manuals for chess as well as IT and lateral thinking. He has also written numerous articles for chess magazines. Bill is an experienced individual and group coach who has a wide and deep understanding of chess. sddsx

www.ingramcontent.com/pod-product-compliance
Lightning Source LLC
LaVergne TN
LVHW041214050326
832903LV00021B/610